MAR 3 0 2017

3 1994 01550 0157

SANTA ANA PUBLIC LIBRARY

D1123918

Save the Bees

THE

with NATURAL BACKYARD HIVES

638.1 MCF
McFarland, Rob
Save the bees with natural
backyard hives

CENTRAL $21.99
                    31994015500157

Save the Bees

WITH NATURAL BACKYARD HIVES

THE EASY AND TREATMENT-FREE WAY
TO ATTRACT AND KEEP HEALTHY BEES

ROB AND
CHELSEA M^cFARLAND

FOUNDERS OF HONEYLOVE.ORG

PAGE STREET
PUBLISHING CO.

PAGE STREET
PUBLISHING CO.

Copyright © 2015 Rob & Chelsea McFarland
First published in 2015 by
Page Street Publishing Co.
27 Congress Street, Suite 103
Salem, MA 01970
www.pagestreetpublishing.com

All rights reserved. No part of this book may be reproduced or used, in any form or by any means,
electronic or mechanical, without prior permission in writing from the publisher.

Distributed by Macmillan; sales in Canada by The Canadian Manda Group.

19   18   17   16   2   3   4   5

ISBN-13: 9781624141416
ISBN-10: 1624141412

Library of Congress Control Number: 2015936978

Cover and book design by Page Street Publishing Co.
Photography by W.B. Fontenot & Rob McFarland

Printed and bound in China

Page Street is proud to be a member of 1% for the Planet. Members donate one percent of their
sales to one or more of the over 1,500 environmental and sustainability charities across the globe
who participate in this program.

DEDICATION

Dedicated to our amazing parents, thank you for all
your love and support!

Mike and Katie McFarland, Amana Nova and
Larry and Leslie Austin.

CONTENTS

The Bees Chose Us

I'm surprised I could hear the bees' buzzing over the work-related stress reverberating through my thoughts as I worked on my garden one spring day. I had taken the day off because it was my birthday, and I needed a day of digging in the dirt to relieve the intense pressure I was feeling. The constant stress of running a technology start-up, and the treachery of power-hungry colleagues was starting to wear on me; I had lost my appetite and slowly started disappearing until I lost over 35 pounds. In a hurry to catch a flight one morning, I pulled on an odd-fitting pair of jeans. It was a lot longer than I'd like to admit before I realized I had squeezed into my wife Chelsea's jeans. That was a face-palm moment if there ever was one! Something needed to change, and fast. Thankfully, I *did* notice the buzzing, and from that moment on our lives have never been the same.

My garden has always served as an antidote to work-related stress and the pressures of modern life. There is something about growing food and working the soil that revitalizes the mind and body in a way that I can't fully describe. It's the perfect medicine for "Nature Deficit Disorder." Nothing strips away angst and anxiety like a few moments of admiring plants and tending your garden. Somehow, as you begin to contemplate the wonders of nature, thoughts about that jerk in traffic or the troll at work suddenly disappear.

I initially noticed a few bees buzzing around my raspberries while getting a raised bed ready for planting. Other than appreciating their free pollination service, I didn't think much of it. I hadn't quite let go of my stress from work when I realized the faint buzzing overhead was growing louder. In what seemed like an instant, thousands of bees appeared out of thin air, and I found myself standing amid a swirling flurry of honeybees. I sensed no cause for alarm, probably because they made no effort to sting me even though I made an easy target. I knew enough about bees to know what was happening, and I darted into the house to retrieve my camera.

I'm not sure what I blurted out as I raced back outside, but it was enough to convince Chelsea that she should close the door quickly behind me. Chelsea had recently been stung multiple times by a vengeful wasp, so seeing me charge outside to willingly surround myself with thousands of stinging insects was enough to make her suspect that I had lost my mind. Meanwhile, I could hardly believe my eyes as I captured footage of the swarm coalescing on a branch in my neighbor's yard. I could hardly stand how interesting the experience was; I suddenly had so many questions about what I was witnessing as I observed this incredible, awe-inspiring swarm of honeybees.

Then, as if I had fallen through thin ice into frigid water, I realized something. The branch the bees selected was directly outside my neighbor's door, and somehow I knew that wasn't going to fly. My worst fears were confirmed when I got in touch with her; she had already placed a call to vector control, and if that didn't work out she would call an exterminator. I managed to reassure her that she wasn't in immediate danger, and convinced her that I would handle it for free.

By pure coincidence, weeks before the swarm arrived, I binge-watched some beekeeping videos on YouTube, and came across a series featuring this crazy—and by crazy I mean awesome—guy from Los Angeles named Kirk Anderson, who went by the name "Kirkobeeo" online. All the other videos I had seen on beekeeping were very earnest and informative, but there was something about Kirk that was so compelling and honest; I just ate up everything he had to say. The videos taught me that swarms were quite docile, and that beekeepers were eager for the opportunity to collect them. Thanks to Kirk I knew exactly what to do when the swarm showed up that day. After Googling how to contact Kirkobeeo, I called the swarm hotline and left an enthusiastic message. I waited impatiently for a beekeeper to return my call. Taking my cues from one of Kirk's videos, I constructed a cardboard swarm box in preparation for the beekeeper's arrival. After what seemed like an eternity—in reality probably two to three hours tops—a beekeeper named Maurice showed up to help relocate the swarm.

We jumped the fence into my neighbor's yard and set up my swarm box under the football-shaped mass of bees festooned from the branch. My neighbor looked on through her window, and wondered out loud when we were going to put on our "beekeeping outfits." I have to admit, the same question occurred to me as Maurice began trimming twigs and branches out of the way just inches from thousands of honeybees. He mumbled something that sounded sort of reassuring, and I was too excited to be overly concerned for my safety, so I just went with it. With one firm snip of the branch, the whole operation was over. The football of bees stayed clustered together as he gently laid them into the open swarm box, and I closed the lid a little quicker than was probably necessary. It was a thrill, and I immediately knew that I wanted more.

Chelsea and I are regularly asked how we got into beekeeping. How did this all start? There is an old saying in beekeeping: "You don't choose to be a beekeeper, the bees choose you." That is most definitely what happened to us!

Since our chance encounter with that swarm, Chelsea and I were swept into this incredibly interesting and mysterious world of honeybees. The swarm was like a flashy lure spinning through the murky water catching the attention of a hungry fish, and we took the bait. Once we learned more about the perils facing bees and beekeepers, the hook was set, and we found ourselves fully committed. The first thing we discovered was that our encounter was not all that unique in Los Angeles. There was in fact a very robust population of feral honeybees—nine to eleven colonies per square mile—living here in America's second-largest city. We also later found out

This book's intention is to provide a how-to primer on an alternative approach to the conventional, chemically based way of beekeeping that is already well-represented in beekeeping literature. When writing about beekeeping, it's not a matter of simply listing a set of actions or procedures. If only it were so easy! Instead, beekeeping, also known as apiculture, is a culture—the collective beliefs, wisdom and practices shared among a subset of people—and has to be described as such. Like any culture, beekeeping has variants or subcultures whose practices and beliefs differ based on location and tradition passed down through the generations and around bee meetings. To reduce this treatment-free variant of beekeeping culture to simply being free of something falls spectacularly short of its mark. Any subculture, philosophy, movement, idea or approach cannot be sustainably defined by opposition; at some point a position must be taken and principles established in order to find identity, purpose and productivity. This book is my attempt to describe a beekeeping subculture not in contrast or opposition, but as a principled set of shared beliefs from which we can build and evolve our understanding of honeybees.

that keeping bees in the city—despite the fact that they were already here—was not allowed under our current city land-use codes. And just like that, we had discovered our mission.

Chelsea and I started HoneyLove to educate and inspire urban beekeepers based on the simple idea that the more people there are who care about bees and pollinators, the better shot we have at saving them for future generations. We figured that if we could inspire people living in cities around the world to welcome bees and beekeepers into their communities, we could help clean up our urban environments, promote sustainable living, advance urban agriculture and empower people with the idea that they can make a difference in their own backyards. The advantage for humans in this bargain is obvious: bees allow us to grow food closer to where we live, and provide us with delicious honey. In exchange, bees get access to some of the best remaining habitat for their hives. It turns out that our urban environments often provide the cleanest and most abundant forage for honeybees. What luck!

As filmmakers and media people, Chelsea and I couldn't resist taking thousands of photos and videos of our newfound source of inspiration. Chelsea began sharing our adventures on social media and youtube.com/HoneyLove, and soon started working on our HoneyLove.org website. It wasn't long before she had set the groundwork for a full-out media campaign to win hearts and minds in support of the much maligned honeybee. Next, she set her sights on legalizing beekeeping in Los Angeles, and connected with Maritza Przekop to start hatching out a plan. Maritza, an LA City Planning Associate and close family friend, was integral to getting farmers markets into West Los Angeles communities a few years prior and had excellent advice for how to organize and focus our efforts. On her suggestion, we launched a grassroots campaign to demonstrate to city officials that their constituents supported beekeeping in their communities.

We started our legalization efforts in our neighborhood by appealing to the community council. To win their support, we launched a six-month feasibility study, and engaged in some colorful and eclectic community outreach. We provided extensive documentation on how other cities around the country have regulated beekeeping, and demonstrated that urban beekeeping is a part of a healthy, sustainable city. Through our outreach at local farmers markets, libraries, schools and community events, we were able to gather a record number of petition signatures. After what seemed at times like an uphill battle, we gained the support of the Mar Vista Community Council. This prompted our city councilman Bill Rosendahl to endorse our motion and urge his fellow city councilmembers to take up the issue.

While the legalization issue continues to work its way through the halls of government—going on four years at the time of this writing—HoneyLove has managed to grow a large community of beekeepers in Los Angeles and create an online presence that spans the globe. One of the most rewarding results of our work has been the feeling of connectedness we get by hearing from beekeepers from all over. Even though we often don't speak the same language, we do share a profound passion for our bees. We have been astonished by the response we have received; we had no idea there were so many people out there who were just as—if not more—crazy about bees! We credit the documentary *Vanishing of the Bees* for raising the public's awareness about honeybees and setting the stage for our work. We now consider the film's director, George Langworthy, among our closest friends. He has become an integral member of HoneyLove.

Vanishing of the Bees taught us that there was something about modern beekeeping that wasn't quite right. For starters, the majority of bees in America are kept in large-scale commercial operations and used to pollinate the nation's food crops. In addition to the stress of having their hives closed up, loaded onto trucks and shipped between farms, these bees have to contend with a different set of pesticides and fungicides on each crop. The health of commercial hives is further compromised by a poor diet of high-fructose corn syrup instead of honey. To add further insult to injury, in order to fend off varroa mites, American foulbrood (AFB) and all manner of infectious microbes, beekeepers have relied on a chemical arsenal of pesticides and antibiotics to "medicate" their hives in recent years.

Something didn't quite add up; how could we expect to treat a colony of *insects* with *insecticides* and hope for a positive outcome? For quite some time, even in the face of irrefutable proof to the contrary, we have heard the same rationale used to explain why the idea of organic agriculture is ridiculous and impossible. We weren't buying it; we knew there had to be another way. Kirk Anderson, the same crazy character who taught me about swarms with his YouTube videos, was there to help guide us in the right direction.

"The thing about smart motherf@*&#rs is that sometimes, they sound like crazy motherf@*&#rs to stupid motherf@*&#rs..."

—Robert Kirkman, *The Walking Dead, Vol. 09:* "Here We Remain"

When presented with the option to treat our bees with pesticides and antibiotics, the choice seemed obvious. We go out of our way to shop for organic foods and we don't use any pesticides in our garden because we don't want to expose our family to potentially harmful chemicals, so why would we intentionally put them in our hives? It made no sense to us to risk contaminating the honey we intended to eat and share with our family and closest friends. Thankfully, we learned early on from Kirk Anderson that there was another way: treatment-free, "backwards" beekeeping.

CHAPTER 1

Principles of Treatment–Free Beekeeping and How It Will Save the Bees

For many beekeepers around the world, the idea of treatment-free beekeeping is taboo—unthinkable even. Beekeeping practices have long been based on the idea that it is impossible to keep honeybees healthy without the use of chemicals. Suggesting an alternative to chemical-laden beekeeping can be met with animosity and dismissal. Treatment-free beekeepers have been shamed with accusations of neglect akin to withholding standard medical treatment from children.

Despite the fact that it has faced modern resistance, treatment-free beekeeping is not a new concept by any measure. For most of human history it would have been simply called "beekeeping." Beekeepers have always fought to protect the purity of their hives and their honey. The idea of putting essential oils, formic acids, oxalic acids, organo-phosphates or any manner of synthetic chemical into the hive would be a perverse thought for the majority of beekeepers throughout history. However, when Varroa destructors (varroa mites) started to hit American hives around 1987, the gloves came off and beekeepers began looking for anything that could help their bees grapple with the destructive parasite. This seek-and-destroy mission quickly escalated into full-out chemical warfare, and has become a protracted struggle for nearly 30 years with no signs of abating any time soon. The sickening reality is that the mites have only become stronger and more resistant to treatments. After three decades, beekeepers must now reflect on whether this has been an effective approach and where do we go from here.

Treatment-free beekeepers believe that chemicals have no place in the hive, and that the "medications" used to fight pests, parasites and diseases only make bees more vulnerable to the very problems they were aimed at solving. The common wisdom in the treatment-free community is that meddling with bees and interfering with the hive is partially responsible for all the issues now facing honeybees. The way forward is to allow our colonies to live in a more natural, less disturbed state. Treatment-free beekeepers place a lot of confidence in their bees' ability to survive and adapt, and believe that bees are resilient enough to grapple with mites and microbes all on their own.

Rather than upending the natural balance of the hive ecology to treat mites, the only sustainable way to combat these common problems is to use the foundational principles of treatment-free beekeeping: maintain strong colonies, use superior genetics and only breed bees that exhibit the hygienic behavior necessary to reduce mite populations. *Reduce* is the operative word here; studies have shown that over time honeybee colonies develop resistance to mites. Treating them with chemicals actually delays or prohibits this adaptation. Hygienic bees are able to smell a brood that is infested with varroa larvae, and remove it from the hive before the mites can spread any farther.

The problem with treating bees is that the chemicals do not discriminate and unfortunately destroy many other beneficial organisms along with their target. A beehive is an ecosystem in and of itself, inhabited by countless microbes, bacteria, fungi and all manner of microscopic life, and held together in a delicate balance worked out over millions of years. By introducing chemicals into this ecosystem, we invariably upset the equilibrium and catalyze a chain of reactions we have barely begun to understand. By treating with chemicals, we interrupt a system that has been solving problems far longer than humans have been traveling around the sun. Treating bees is an attempt to cheat evolution, and in fact has an adverse effect, making evolutionary pressures even greater.

You cannot eliminate every mite or every spore when you treat your bees, and those remaining mites and spores actually evolve to evade and resist your chemicals. The mites that aren't killed by the treatment go on to reproduce and pass on whatever genetic advantage allowed them to survive the beekeeper's previous treatments. In essence, rather than breeding stronger bees you are breeding mites that are stronger and more treatment-resistant with every generation.

Treatment-free beekeeper inspecting the hive (Right)

Treatments have had their place in beekeeping, but it is imperative that we find better solutions. In order to develop more resilient bees, the unfortunate truth is that we have to let a whole lot of weak bees perish. The longer we keep propping up weaker bees on the chemical treadmill, the longer we delay the inevitable—all the while making our enemies stronger. That said, we can't ask our commercial beekeepers whose operations are responsible for pollinating the majority of our food to take such a massive risk without setting up every possible safety net, and to date there exist no such protections for beekeepers to take that massive financial gamble.

This is where our opportunity to make a difference as small-scale beekeepers comes into play. Most of you reading this book will likely never become commercial-level beekeepers and only wish to participate as a hobby. This is not to say you take it any less seriously, only that your entire income will *not* be based on beekeeping, pollination services, honey sales and so on. Hobby beekeepers whose businesses and mortgages are not tied to annual colony losses or honey production can afford to take the risks necessary to buck the chemical way of beekeeping. Again, this does not mean that we have any less responsibility when it comes to dealing with disease and keeping our bees healthy; it just means that we have the flexibility to take risks and be experimental.

There is a parallel to the technology industry here. You have the tech giants like Google, Apple and Microsoft who have all the money, infrastructure, brain power and market advantage, yet it is often the kid in his dorm room who comes up with the greatest innovations simply because he is afforded the flexibility to think freely and tinker without consideration of running a business, satisfying shareholders or paying out yearly dividends. Going with the Mark Zuckerberg model here, the smaller-scale beekeeper has the flexibility to test, experiment and bring other skills and perspectives to the table. With that flexibility comes the distinct possibility of hitting it big and changing the industry as a whole. It would be foolhardy for the commercial beekeeping industry to do anything but welcome beekeepers of every stripe with open arms, as it stands to benefit most from the solutions brought on by new ways of thinking.

BEEKEEPING BACKWARDS

The principles of beekeeping backwards were first articulated by an observant and humble beekeeper named Charles Martin Simon in an issue of *Bee Culture* from 2001. While Simon didn't get into the to-treat or not-to-treat debate, he did give us a convenient framework to define "beekeeping backwards."

Eggs, open brood and capped brood (Left)

CHARLES MARTIN SIMON'S
TEN PRINCIPLES OF BEEKEEPING BACKWARDS

Principle #1: Work with Nature, not against Her.

Principle #2: Profit doesn't mean a whole heck of a lot if you're dead.

Principle #3: Dead bees make no honey.

Principle #4: Don't fight it.

Principle #5: Beekeeping is not about honey.

Principle #6: It's not about money.

Principle #7: It's about survival.

Principle #8: Forget everything you ever learned and start observing what is really going on.

Principle #9: Leave your bees alone.

Principle #10: Leave me alone.

The ideas gained further traction when appropriated by Kirk Anderson who evangelized the ideas to the swelling ranks of Los Angeles urban beekeepers. Kirk's free-spirited attitude, hands-off approach and wicked sense of humor resonated with a set of rebel beekeepers who already identified with the impulse to buck convention. This loosely affiliated group of people came to call themselves the "Backwards Beekeepers™" and were soon overrun with eager "newbees" seeking answers and community—your humble authors included. Perhaps Kirk's greatest legacy is his insistence on an additional principle.

Principle #11: Beekeeping should be fun.

This is a helpful reminder for beekeepers fretting about mites or falling victim to warnings of doom and gloom.

Kirk's obvious love of bees encouraged countless new beekeepers, and his approach made beekeeping accessible and appealing to a whole new generation of beekeepers. Along with fellow treatment-free beekeepers like Ed and Dee Lusby, Michael Bush, Sam Comfort, Les Crowder, Laurie Herboldsheimer, Dean Stiglitz, Michael Thiele and many others, Kirk served as a whistle-blower alerting beekeepers around the world that rethinking our practices was critical to the future of bees. While the ideas behind backwards beekeeping do not belong to Mr. Simon, Mr. Anderson or any beekeeper for that matter, both men deserve tremendous credit for their contributions to the conversation about beekeeping.

Like "treatment-free beekeeping," the term "beekeeping backwards" still does not serve as the catch-all term describing all of the ideas, opinions and practices of this variant of apiculture. "Organic" falls apart as well when you delve into the details of what treatments are allowed under a USDA-sanctioned license use of the term. "All-natural" fails for similar reasons, namely that many treatments allowed under this label are of "naturally occurring" chemicals like oxalic acid. One main decision sets beekeepers with the same end goal on opposing paths—whether or not to use chemical treatments. This is probably the most consequential, far-reaching decision a beekeeper must make. Due to the divergent course of action beekeepers take depending on this choice, labeling the opposing schools of thought, even if inadequate, is necessary.

FIRST STEP– UNDERSTANDING OUR BEES

Despite what critics often allege, treatment-free beekeeping is not anti-science. Rather than looking for chemicals to circumvent the rules of nature, treatment-free beekeeping calls for a far more comprehensive scientific approach to understand the massively complex systems at work in a beehive. Honeybee colonies are infinitely more complex than our current understanding suggests. The rules of the hive may be so abstract that we lack the vocabulary to adequately describe its complexity, much less understand it.

Our current understanding of honeybees is similar to the common beliefs surrounding disease before the germ theory of disease was introduced. People dropping dead was much easier to blame on evil spirits at play rather than the work of invisible microbes. There were no common words at the time for the masses to describe things like germs, viruses and infectious bacteria, and therefore no way for people to understand the concepts and incorporate them into their cultural narrative. Germs were not part of the collective imagination, and it wasn't until their machinations were unlocked and described that we understood that the complexity of life was far greater than ever imagined.

Our current knowledge of how things work within the hive is akin to our understanding of infectious disease during the 1700s. We lack adequate language to describe the complexity of systems and feedback loops at work in the hive, and therefore must make a set of primitive assumptions based on what little data we are able to interpret. The assumptions about the hive underpinning modern apiculture are based on incomplete data, and the resulting beekeeping practices deliberately subvert honeybees' natural systems and behaviors in service of increased honey production and purely economic considerations.

A better understanding of bees can lead to better beekeeping practices, which in turn can help make our agricultural system less lethal to bees and less destructive to our ecosystems. This all starts by simply owning up to the fact that the current system isn't working and our understanding of the world is incomplete. We must abandon the dogma that rejects new ideas and unlearn what we think we know in order to approach the problems facing beekeepers with fresh eyes and open minds.

The hope for the future of beekeeping may be supercomputing. In the same way these powerful supercomputers are used to understand the systems governing the Earth, scientists can now begin to use advanced computer modeling to understand the complexity at play in the hive. In the meantime, beekeepers can only abandon the treatments that are disruptive to the hive ecology and the natural systems responsible for the health and prosperity of the colony.

As Michael Bush, author of *The Practical Beekeeper: Beekeeping Naturally,* said in a video interview I shot for HoneyLove's YouTube Channel:

"A bee colony isn't really just a bunch of bees that live together. It is a whole ecology. It is 8,000 microorganisms and 30 different kinds of mites and at least 30 different kinds of insects and all sorts of fungi and bacteria that all live together in this ecology that we call a bee colony. And treating pretty much ignores that that even exists and then it disrupts the entire balance of that colony. The entire balance of that ecology is dependent on things being in a balance, where you have a whole bunch of different microorganisms that keep each other from taking over. This is obvious in an organism, but people tend to forget that a colony is a super-organism. So it's not just the things that live in the gut of the bee. It's things that live in the beebread, which is the pollen that they're fermenting. It's the things that live in the colony and under the colony and the detritus that falls on the bottom. There's this whole ecology that's many more organisms than a bee and when you treat you disrupt that whole thing."

Honeybee collecting nectar (Right)

CHAPTER 2

Beekeeping Basics: Getting Started Is Easy and Fun

Beekeeping is perhaps the most addictive activity one can discover. For centuries beekeepers have described the powerful hold honeybees have on them as "bee fever." Though not literally a communicable disease, beekeepers around the world describe similar symptoms—primarily an all-encompassing passion for these winged wonders. Once new beekeepers come down with a case of the bee fever, honey and bees practically take over their every thought. Before long, new beekeepers start pouring over books and YouTube videos in their spare hours, dreaming of their hive buzzing with bees. Established beekeepers are all familiar with the routine: the "newbee"

is exposed to the seduction of the hive and all of a sudden can't wait another second before getting bees and becoming a beekeeper. Predictably, the first question every newbee breathlessly asks is, "How do I get started?" This is quickly followed by, "And when do I get to harvest honey!?!"

To embark on the beekeeping journey, one must acquire three crucial things: community, education and equipment.

COMMUNITY

Just like honeybees, beekeepers cannot exist without community. Whether it is an online community, a local beekeeping association or just a handful of mentors, a beekeeper needs to benefit from the collective wisdom of the greater beekeeping community. These groups are essential for sharing the resources and knowledge necessary to navigate the world of honeybees.

The ancient art of apiculture is the manifestation of the collective intellectual achievement of beekeepers stretching back over 8,000 years. This legacy would be impossible had beekeepers not been fastidious record keepers of their observations and experiences. By becoming a beekeeper, you are signing up to build on and carry forward a body of knowledge with a tradition as old as humanity.

It cannot be overstated how important education is to beekeeping, but at the same time one should not be discouraged by the amount there is to learn. Beekeeping is filled with such wonder and excitement that soaking up the knowledge becomes addicting and fun, which accelerates the learning process. Beekeepers are encouraged to join as many beekeeping communities, forums, associations and clubs as possible. Just like bees, beekeepers need one another to share knowledge and resources.

For a list of beekeeping clubs, resources and websites, visit: HoneyLove.org/resources.

EDUCATION

You can cover the basics of beekeeping with a modest amount of reading. That said, no single book can hope to fully capture the complexity of honeybees or provide a comprehensive guide to every beekeeping strategy. Much of beekeeping is an art, which is to say, each individual can tailor the finer aspects of beekeeping to suit his or her unique relationship with honeybees. To develop your own techniques and creative solutions, beekeepers are encouraged to read up on how others have approached the same problems and not be limited to any one way of thinking. With that in mind, new beekeepers do not have to know everything there is to know about the ancient craft before getting bees. Sometimes you have to learn by doing and cannot fully understand the process until, as Chelsea likes to say, you're "getting your hands sticky." It is to your advantage to find a mentor who will help guide you along the way, and it's a good idea to get firsthand experience with bees before making the financial investments necessary to keep them.

New beekeepers need both a conceptual understanding of beekeeping and hands-on experience. (Left)

EQUIPMENT

The third critical step to becoming a beekeeper is acquiring the necessary equipment. Getting bees without the proper gear is potentially dangerous to the beekeeper and harmful to the bees. Beekeepers need to have all the equipment ready to go when their swarm, package of bees or nucleus colony arrives. There is a fair amount of investment needed to get going, so it is important to be familiar with the equipment to make informed purchasing decisions. Again, based on scale and approach, equipment requirements can vary from beekeeper to beekeeper. This book will focus on the needs of a small-scale beekeeper and is not meant to sufficiently describe the needs of a commercial-scale beekeeper.

A TREATMENT-FREE BEEKEEPER'S FIRST YEAR EQUIPMENT CHECKLIST

- *Hiveware*
  - *hive boxes – $25 each*
  - *bottom board – $15*
  - *top board – $15*
  - *frames – $3 each*
- *Weatherproofing – $20*
- *Starter Strips – $10*
- *Protective Clothing*
  - *suit – $100*
  - *veil – $35*
  - *gloves – $25*
- *Smoker – $25*
- *Hive Tool – $15*
- *Savvy*
- *Patience*

Approximate Total – $500

The standard hive—or the sum of the hiveware—is generally composed from the ground up of one bottom board, two deep hive boxes, one to three medium hive boxes, one top board and 10-frames in each of the hive boxes. This equals twenty deep frames and ten to thirty medium frames. This should be sufficient hiveware for a colony's first year. In the event that beekeepers find some exceptional bees and hit a number of strong nectar flows, it is possible that a first-year colony will expand beyond the boxes they have on hand—but that is a really great "problem" to have. In the first year, the majority of hives are unlikely to produce a large enough surplus of honey that can be safely harvested, especially in a cold climate where the bees will need the honey to survive the winter.

HIVE DESIGNS

Around the world, bees are kept in a variety of structures, from the highly manufactured Langstroth hive to more natural structures like hollow logs, gums, straw skeps and earthenware pots. In the United States, beekeepers are required to keep their bees in hives with movable frames like the Langstroth hive that allow the beekeepers to selectively manage the honeycombs and inspect for diseases like American foulbrood (see p. 100). This policy rules out the use of logs, pots or skeps because of their lack of movable frames, and as a result the Langstroth hive was widely adopted as the standard beehive design for American beekeepers.

The Langstroth hive was designed and patented by Reverend Lorenzo Lorraine Langstroth in 1852. It is a modular design, which allows the beekeeper to add more hive boxes when the bees are expanding or to remove them when it's time to harvest honey or consolidate space. Hive boxes are filled with movable wooden frames that allow the beekeeper to efficiently inspect the honeycombs within each frame with minimal impact on the hive. If properly spaced, frames in a Langstroth hive allow for perfect "bee space" between combs.

The specific dimensions for the Langstroth hive were created to accommodate "bee space" or the spatial rules that bees follow in the construction of their hive. In the 1800s Reverend Langstroth observed that anywhere his bees had more than ⅜ inch to move around in, they would fill the space with comb. Each comb is spaced at least ⅜ inch, which allows two bees to easily move past each other on neighboring combs. Whereas areas in the hive smaller than ⅜ inch are packed with propolis, or "bee glue," a sticky mixture of plant resins that bees collect to fortify the hive structure and protect against various non-beneficial microbes such as viruses, bacteria, fungi and other would-be invaders such as ants, hive beetles, wax moths and mites.

Langstroth hives have ⅜-inch spaces between combs.

The other well-known movable frame hive design is called the Kenyan top-bar hive. Developed by Dr. Maurice V. Smith and Dr. Gordon Townsend from the University of Guelph in Canada for the Canadian International Development Agency, top-bars were adopted by the Peace Corps as a low-cost alternative for beekeeping projects in the developing world. Keeping bees in a top-bar can be a wonderful experience for both bees and beekeeper and is probably the most cost-effective movable-frame hive. You can make top-bars out of all kinds of material—from mud and wicker to plastic barrels and scrap wood—and with just a little creativity and some rudimentary carpentry skills you can make a hive that will cost you next to nothing. Les Crowder, a highly regarded treatment-free beekeeper, wrote the gold standard book on top-bar beekeeping, appropriately titled *Top-Bar Beekeeping: Organic Practices for Honeybee Health*. Les has taught top-bar beekeeping in many parts of the world where keeping bees in Langstroth hives is impractical and prohibitively expensive. For free top-bar hive designs, please visit: HoneyLove .org/Resources.

In an interview for the HoneyLove YouTube channel, Les told me that "the best teachers of beekeeping are your own bees, and it's kind of a matter of hours of getting your hands in the beehive and using your eyes, ears, nose—smelling [and] observing as best you can and seeing what effect what you do has on them, and learn how to be calm around them and look at them." For Les the appeal of top-bar beekeeping is that the bees draw all of their own wax combs, and he feels the design allows him to have a more natural and gentle relationship with his bees.

Both designs have their advantages and disadvantages, but this book will primarily focus on Langstroth hives due to their ubiquity and the fact that they have a standard size throughout the world. Whichever hive design you are keeping your bees in, all of the same basic principles of treatment-free beekeeping apply. The only difference between the two is how the beekeeper manages space within the hive. Because top-bar hives have a finite amount of room for the bees to expand their colonies, it means that you have to remove combs to create space; with a Langstroth you can always just add another box

Top-bar hive with observation window (Above)
Top-bar hive with naturally drawn comb (Right)

to create space for the colony's expansion. Langstroths are a bit more forgiving of mistakes and poor technique, which is valuable for new beekeepers. This is a greater consideration for new urban beekeepers who have to be extra cautious about upsetting their bees and potentially getting people or pets stung. For this reason, I generally recommend new beekeepers learn the basics with a Langstroth and eventually get a top-bar later on so you can compare and contrast the two designs. If your bees are far from neighbors and animals, you can afford to be more experimental without fear of stings and you can try whatever hive design your heart desires.

LANGSTROTH HIVES—LEARNING THE LINGO

Like any hobby it can take a little while to pick up the jargon and lingo of beekeeping, but fortunately most item names are derivative of their function or size. Some of the words in beekeeping only have meaning after you have seen it up close for yourself. Once you make that visual connection you can learn the vocabulary very quickly. To inform your purchasing decisions, you should first familiarize yourself with the equipment you'll need to purchase.

HIVE BOXES

Hive boxes—the wooden boxes designed specifically to be stacked on top of each other and filled with wooden frames—come in three main sizes:

"Deeps" are the largest box and are primarily used to host the hive's brood nest[1]—the womb-like portion of the hive where the queen lays her eggs. (See p. 93.)

"Mediums" or "Supers" are, as the name would imply, the mid-level-size hive box primarily used for honey storage, but they are also used as the brood nest to make them lighterweight and more manageable. The word "super" means "on top of," which in this context means on top of the brood nest where the bees are likely to store their honey.

"Shallows," as the highly creative name illuminates, are the smallest or shallowest of the hive boxes used for supering and cut-comb honey production—honey pulled straight from the hive and sold still enclosed in the raw honeycombs.

To add to the confusion, each of these depth sizes also comes in 8-frame and 10-frame width options. Beekeepers with bad backs or those who have many stairs to climb often prefer 8-frame setups because they are considerably lighter—approximately sixty to seventy pounds—when laden with honeycomb as compared to their 10-frame counterparts—eighty to ninety pounds. You can shave an additional ten to twenty pounds off of each box by using mediums, which would make each box weigh between fifty to sixty pounds.

---

1   The brood nest is the womb-like portion of the beehive where honeybee embryos go through the various stages of development: eggs, larvae and pupae.

"Deep" frame from Langstroth hive without foundation (Left)

FRAMES

Frames come in three sizes to match the hive box sizes: shallow, medium and deep. If ordering online, be sure to check that your frames are appropriately sized to fit the boxes. The frames rest on a ledge inside the hive box so that the top bar of the frame sits flush with the top of the box. This allows the beekeeper to stack hive boxes on top of each other as the colony grows, and exchange frames between boxes to help build the colony upward. Frames also allow the beekeeper to manage space to prevent overcrowding, which might otherwise result in swarming or increased defensive behavior.

Unassembled frames come in four pieces with three parts: one top bar, one bottom bar and two side bars. New beekeepers often prefer to purchase slightly more expensive assembled frames to save themselves the time and effort it takes to nail them together. Using a beekeeping tool called a "frame jig" or something similar that can hold the wooden parts in place can speed up assembly time, and employing a compressed air-staple gun can save you from accidentally hammering your thumbs. If you use staples, you may also want to use a nail or two and a dab of nontoxic wood glue for added strength before stapling.

BOTTOM BOARD

The bottom board is—you guessed it—the board that goes on the bottom of the hive. The bottom of the bottom board has wooden strips that serve as feet and keep the hive a ½-inch off the ground. The top of the bottom board, which faces the inside of the hive, has ¼-inch risers on three sides that raise the hive boxes off the bottom board, leaving a ¼-inch gap across the front edge. The bees will use the gap as their entrance and exit from the hive. Toward the end of the year, you can reduce the entrance down to just a few inches to allow the bees to more easily defend the hive from "robber bees." These are outside honeybees that attempt to forcibly steal honey from the hive. I like to keep the entrance permanently reduced to limit the number of guard bees required to fend off intruders. Nearly all of the feral bees I've removed from structures like walls and water meters only have entrances big enough for two bees to fit through at a time. I screw or nail my bottom boards into my bottom boxes to prevent them from coming apart when moved.

Beekeeper placing an entrance reducer on a hive. This helps the bees to more easily defend the hive. (Right)

Entrance reducers help hives fend off robber bees.

Many beekeepers use screened bottom boards, which use a screen in lieu of wood for most of the bottom board. This encourages air flow and allows mites and other potential pests to fall out of the hive. The problem is that it also lets them in, and gives the bees a larger surface area to guard. To split the difference, I prefer to cut a 1½-inch hole in the bottom of a solid bottom board and cover it with hardware cloth. This does two things: it allows for ventilation and it gives the bees somewhere to trap and discard pests.

TOP BOARD

Top boards are the final basic component of a Langstroth hive. Top boards provide a roof to shelter the hive from the elements, and of course, help keep all of the colony's resources and bees *inside* the hive. The top board is also the beekeeper's entrance to the hive. Each time a hive is inspected or opened, the beekeeper must first remove the top board to gain access to the hive.

Distributing the colony through additional lighter boxes can make a hive much more manageable for people who don't want to or can't hoist a ninety-pound box from the ground. To prevent potential injuries, it pays to familiarize oneself with the fundamentals of good lifting form and technique. Practice lifting empty hive boxes "with your legs" before trying it out in the field surrounded by bees; your back will thank you later. Beekeeping requires a certain amount of strength—mostly mental, but also a fair amount of physical strength is needed to move heavy equipment around. The good news is that one of the best parts of beekeeping is getting to share the unique experiences with others, so even if you cannot manage the physical responsibilities personally, you can still participate in this amazing hobby by bringing someone on board who is up for an adventure and capable of lugging a heavy box from time to time. It's advisable to consult with your doctor if your health and fitness is a concern or if you are allergic to stings before diving into beekeeping.

Top boards are generally flat with caps on the front and back that help keep the top board firmly in place. Alternatively, beekeepers can use a system that is a combination of an inner cover and a telescoping top or migratory cover. These are designed for colder climates where snow might sit on top of the hive for months at a time. The metal tops prevent moisture from sneaking through. An argument can also be made for better ventilation and decreased condensation during the cold and wet months. That said, a simple wooden top board can be equally effective and is typically less expensive than the two-piece system.

WEATHERPROOFING

Before installing bees into hiveware, it is important for the beekeeper to weatherproof the outside of the hive. The bees don't care if their hive boxes are rotting and falling apart—they might actually like it better! However, weatherproofing extends the life of your hive boxes, and saves you the expense of having to replace deteriorating boxes. For the majority of beekeepers, weatherproofing means painting the outside of their boxes, top and bottom boards with white paint. This also helps the bees regulate hive temperature by reflecting sunlight and heat.

The essential weatherproofing supplies are raw linseed oil, pure beeswax, a melting pot and a paintbrush.

Most outdoor paints help preserve the wood, however treatment-free beekeepers worry about the paint chemical's impact on their hives. Bees are incredibly sensitive to chemicals and odors, and fresh paint smell can discourage bees from sticking with their new location. Beekeepers are advised to paint their hives well in advance so that fumes have time to dissipate. Paint is also known to release the gas trapped by the paint. Paint offgassing is known to affect indoor air quality in human homes. The effect of paint offgassing on honeybee colonies is unknown and likely immeasurable. Chances are, the offgass will not knock down the hive, but it probably places some amount of stress on the colony. When possible, you should remove any unnecessary stress or burden on the hive.

There fortunately is a great do-it-yourself alternative to paint that we use on our hives. The combination of raw linseed oil, beeswax and propolis painted on the outside of hive woodenware is one of the best ways to protect the equipment while being sensitive to the bees' vulnerabilities. Follow the steps below:

1. Add old combs and/or wax cappings and propolis to a kettle, pot or crock pot and heat until fully melted. Always be attentive when melting wax to prevent fire or injury, no matter how unlikely. Don't worry about filtering out slumgum[1], bee parts or any residual hive products.

2. Slowly add in equal parts raw linseed oil and stir until well mixed (e.g., 6 cups linseed oil with 6 cups wax).

3. This combination can be applied directly to the wood while in liquid form, or poured into a vessel to cool to be used later as a rub. Using the combination as a rub is a more efficient use of resources, but also requires a great deal more effort to apply. Once the mix has cooled down, it can be rubbed into the wood with rags. Painting with liquid wax is messy and has the potential to cause burns, but it gets the job done much faster. Lay down tarps or newspapers to help with cleanup, and use a pair of old pants and closed-toed shoes to prevent splashed wax from scalding exposed skin.

FORGOING FOUNDATIONS

One thing you won't find on the treatment-free beekeeper's hive checklist is wax foundations—thin wax sheets with hexagonal impressions. Foundations have been standard issue for Langstroth hives since 1857, and are designed to serve as the pattern for the bees to follow in constructing their wax cells. These cells are like wombs for brood, or baby bees, and serve as brewing vats for pollen and nectar, which become brood food and honey, respectively, after fermentation.

The argument for using a foundation is that it keeps your combs nice and straight, making it *much* easier to inspect and work the hive. Additionally, it is argued that by providing the foundation, you save the bees' resources and energy, which could otherwise be put toward honey production.

Yes, having perfectly straight combs is convenient for a variety of reasons, but whether they are in the best interest of the bees is highly debatable. Beehives found in natural settings like trees, logs, caves and natural cavity spaces *never* feature combs built in perfectly straight lines. If left to their own devices, bees will build wavy combs that wrap around each other and intersect in a sort of organized asymmetry. Bees will use the available space for maximum storage capacity and do not value the strict order we humans seek to impose.

Without manmade foundations, bees build cells of varying sizes—from 4.6 mm to 5.1 mm for regular worker brood and honey storage. By design, foundations create a uniform cell size—5.4 mm—that the bees must use for everything from brood rearing to food storage. In nature, bees use a variety of sizes to suit different purposes. For example, drones, or male bees, require a much larger cell—6.4 mm to 6.6 mm—to

---

1   Slumgum is the residual substance left after rendering beeswax comprised of cocoons, propolis and other debris from within the hive.

accommodate their pupation. Therefore, bees designate areas specifically for drone brood production called drone comb. The uniformity of foundation discourages but does not prevent drone production—bees will just chew away the foundation and draw their own wax for drone comb.

"I call myself the permissive beekeeper; I let them build whatever they want. I figure how would I know what's the right cell size? My bees don't try to regress me into small shoes—they let me wear whatever size I want, so I'm going to let them live in whatever size they want. What's wrong with letting them have what they want? In other words, we should let bees do their own thing, be their own selves and let them thrive in that way."[1]

—Les Crowder

Bees in feral colonies will use a variety of cell sizes to store honey and use significantly smaller cells to rear worker, or non-reproductive female, brood. As a result, feral bees are noticeably smaller than their foundation-raised counterparts. In tinkering with foundations and, as always, looking for ways to get even greater yields from bees, beekeepers discovered that if they made the hexagonal impressions slightly larger, the bees would draw slightly larger cells—5.4 mm. Larger cells were obviously better for honey storage, but the perceived benefit was that the larger cells allowed for more room for pupation, which in turn produced a larger bee. Bigger cell equals bigger bee, which equals more honey and more money, which equals a better bee—or so the thinking went.

The extent to which this has been debunked can be debated, but in many cases this innovation seems to have resulted in bees that are more vulnerable to certain pests. For example, the tracheal mite preys upon honeybees by laying eggs within the bee's trachea where they hatch and go on to feast on bee blood, haemolymph. The foundation-raised bees with their larger tracheae or spiracles seem to have a harder time keeping mites from entering and reproducing. Taking their cues from feral bees' preference for smaller cells for raising brood, many organic and treatment-free beekeepers have regressed their bee cells down from 5.4 mm to around 4.9 mm to help their bees reduce the number of mites in their hives. Backwards beekeepers ditch the foundation altogether, and let bees draw all of their own comb and use whatever size cell they want.

One reason backwards beekeepers forgo foundations is the fact that the beeswax used in foundations is contaminated with pesticides used to treat hives in the commercial beekeeping operations. All the recycled wax used to make foundations is sourced from commercial operations, thus ensuring that it has been exposed to chemicals from treatments and pesticides.

1   Les Crowder, HoneyLove YouTube Video: Top-Bar Keeping— http://youtu.be/X7ymxFM5TUo

New combs being drawn on a foundationless Langstroth frame. (Left)

Virtually all of the synthetic chemicals, organic acids and essential oils used in conventional beekeeping are "lipophilic," which is to say they are attracted to and dissolved in lipids or fats. Wax is a fat, which means these chemicals become infused in the combs and contaminate the hive at its core. By starting a colony with contaminated foundations, beekeepers introduce chemicals, which would otherwise never be found within the hive.

STARTER STRIPS

Foundationless beekeepers do not have to sacrifice all order or inspectability when they forgo foundations. Instead, you can create starter strips to encourage the bees to draw their own comb within the frames. If you already purchased frames with foundations, the easiest way to create a starter strip is to cut them down to below the first line of foundation wire, and use the rest to make candles or to treat woodenware.[1] This leaves just enough foundation to set them up building in straight lines. Obviously this doesn't remove all the contaminated wax and all that comes with it, but it does drastically reduce the degree to which the hive is contaminated. The trade-off to perfectly straight combs is enough to satisfy all but the most hardcore treatment-free beekeepers.

Another way to create starter strips or "comb guides" is to place tongue depressors in the groove on the underside of the top bar and brush on a thin layer of clean wax. For added strength, use a non-toxic glue like Elmer's® to hold the tongue depressors in place. For the record, starter strips will not force bees to draw straight combs; they simply serve to encourage them in the right direction. It is entirely possible that the bees will draw cross comb,[2] which in turn makes it impossible to remove affected frames without cutting through combs. This is a real drag and should be avoided if possible.

In order to prevent cross comb, beekeepers must regularly inspect their hives, at least every three weeks during spring buildup, and gently correct combs that have gone off course with a sharp knife or hive tool, using rubber bands to hold them in place. Once the bees have drawn a straight comb, it is much easier to set them on course to draw the next one in similar fashion.

---

1 The excess wax from commercial foundations is not recommended to use for lip balms and salves as it contains the recycled commercial chemicals from past beekeeping operations.

2 Cross comb is when bees deviate from the frame and build their combs across multiple frames.

Brushing beeswax on a starter strip (Opposite page—top left)

Bees drawing comb from a starter strip (Opposite page—top right)

Two frames with starter strips and one with a traditional foundation cut down to starter-strip size (Opposite page—bottom)

PROTECTIVE CLOTHING

Next to the required woodenware, perhaps the most important purchase a new beekeeper must make is a quality bee suit. As anyone, myself included, who has had to go to work with comically swollen lips can attest, being stung in the face is no fun.

Over millions of years of evolution, honeybees developed an extremely potent sense of smell that allows them to detect would-be marauders like bears, honey badgers and humans. Bees can detect the exhaled CO_2, which triggers a defensive response from the hive. For instance, a hungry bear sniffing around a beehive is going to trip the hive's CO_2 alarm, resulting in guard bees rushing out to deter the bear with stings to the nose, mouth, eyes and ears. If you attempt to inspect your hive without a suit, you can expect the same deterrent response.

Bee suits are by no means sting-proof, but drastically reduce the potential for stings. There are several types of suits, from veiled pith helmets to full coveralls with integrated veils. The main consideration is whether they will keep bees out of your face, while giving you the necessary confidence to work a hive. Simple veiled pith helmets are easy to take on and off, and meet the basic requirement of keeping bees out of your face, but offer little to no protection for the rest of your body.

Integrated veils come in two basic designs: the English-style "fencing" or "domed" hood, which resembles a hoodie sweatshirt, and, my personal favorite, a round veil that has a brimmed hat with 360-degree visibility—eyes in the back of your head not included. Both varieties can be paired with either a half-jacket or full coveralls. The main advantage of the hoodie-type veil is easy storage; you can compress the whole suit without fear of damaging the netted area. Domed veils do not compress well and the more rigid netting can get bent out of shape fairly easily. Whichever veil design you choose, it is a good idea to wear a hat or baseball cap underneath to keep the netting away from your skin.

Bee suits are typically white because bees have a tendency to behave more aggressively toward dark colors. Also, a white suit makes it easier to spot any six-legged hitchhikers before disrobing. While experienced beekeepers with ultra-docile bees can be seen on YouTube and in demonstrations working their bees without any suit at all, new beekeepers should never attempt working their bees without full protective gear.

Three bee suit and veil options (Left-top)

Veiled pith helmet (Left-bottom)

"Fencing" or "domed"-hood veil (Top)

Round veil (Bottom)

GLOVES

Gloves are an extension of the bee suit, and while not strictly mandatory they help give new beekeepers the confidence needed to reach their hands into a hive packed with 50,000 bees. Gloves are made of rubber, cloth or leather and each material has its advantages and disadvantages. Rubber gloves are easiest to clean, but are the hottest and least breathable option. Cloth is highly breathable, but offers the least resistance to stings. Leather gloves are breathable and highly sting resistant, but are hard to clean and can absorb potential contaminants. Experienced beekeepers (myself included) often eschew gloves altogether for optimal dexterity, comfort and cleanliness. This requires a high degree of confidence and understanding of bee behavior, and therefore is not recommended for new beekeepers. I always bring a pair of leather gloves just in case my bees insist on stinging my hands, which although rare does happen occassionally.

PANT CUFFS AKA "THE DANGER ZONE"

The first beekeeping lesson many of us learn is that the most vulnerable place for accidental stings is the pant cuff. Often during inspections, for one reason or another, bees get bumped off their comb and end up on the ground. Commonly these are young bees that have yet to leave the hive or are just venturing out for the first time. Instinctively these fallen bees begin to climb the nearest vertical structure—your legs—in the hopes of rejoining the hive. If you're not wearing boots or have not in some way accounted for the gap between your shoe and pant cuff, you are likely to get stung in the ankles as bees get caught up in your socks.

Glove options: leather, rubber or cloth

Zippered pant leg of a bee suit

Experienced beekeepers have all done this and can recognize it instantly; we call it the beekeeper dance. It goes something like this: panic sets in when you realize that stinging insects are crawling inside your pants, you begin slapping at your ankles in a futile but hilarious effort to squash any would-be stingers, and with each slap and resulting sting your legs begin to flail faster until you have worked yourself into a slap-happy fury of "ants in your pants" gyrations as you gallop away from the hive, your pride barely in tow.

Joking aside, it is a good idea to take precautions to prevent unnecessary stings. Boots or high-tops are recommended as they go a long way toward preventing ankle stings. Wool socks provide some additional protection. You can purchase special ankle protectors—beekeeper spats—or Velcro bands to keep your pant cuff closed off, but rubber bands work just as well. Duct tape is another great low-cost option, but will leave an ugly adhesive on your shoes, if you care about that sort of thing.

An integrated veil with full coveralls, gloves, proper footwear and the like offer you as much protection against stings as is possible, but as mentioned, there is no way to fully make yourself sting-proof. Beekeeper error and accidental contact are the most common reason for stings. With time and experience you can cut down on the likelihood of both. Typically it does not take long for beekeepers to learn from their mistakes; bees have an excellent way of providing you with instant feedback that they do not approve of your technique. The best way to limit stings is to work your bees with calm, deliberate movements and spare them any unnecessary disruption. Good technique and thoughtful beekeeping will result in fewer stings and a more enjoyable experience for you and your bees.

SMOKER

When bees sense smoke in the air, the first thing you notice is a dramatic shift in the tone of the bees' buzzing as the information is communicated throughout the hive. Almost immediately, bees turn their attention to gorging on honey and nectar. Bees can be observed with their heads buried in open cells eating as much energy-rich food as possible. It is theorized that this is an innate survival instinct with bees reckoning "where there is smoke, there is fire." If there is a fire that threatens the structure housing the hive, the bees will have to evacuate, or abscond, in a hurry and find a new cavity space to colonize. In order to start the colony over, the bees will need as many of the resources as they can salvage from their previous hive to improve their chances of survival.

Considering bees have separate stomachs for transporting nectar back to the hive, in theory bees should be able to take some of their food stores with them. We cannot be certain if this is the case or if smoke just gives them the munchies, but

A smoker is a beekeeper's best friend. (Right)

The smoker is the beekeeper's best friend and likely has been for at least 8,000 years. Why? Well, the simple answer is because smoke allows beekeepers to work the bees without causing themselves or the bees undo harm. The Araña Caves of Valencia, Spain, feature 8,000-year-old epipaleolithic artwork depicting the "Man of Bicorp" climbing vines to raid a wild beehive. While we cannot be certain, some beekeepers looking at the rudimentary rock art get the impression that the raider was supported by smoke rising from a strategically placed fire below. It almost looks like the honey hunter is holding some sort of primitive smoker—or maybe it's a bucket for the plundered honey. The figure's curvy body suggests that it might not be the "man" of Bicorp at all; it's just as likely to have been a woman smoking those bees and bringing home the honey!

No matter what you see in our ancestor's artwork, it is fair to say that early humans were capable of making the same observations of honeybee behavior as we are today. They likely noticed that the presence of smoke changed the bees' behavior in a couple of helpful ways.

what we do know is that smoke refocuses the bees' attention from defending the hive to eating honey. Additionally, smoke disrupts the bees' ability to properly communicate. Bees rely on their incredible sense of smell to interpret the pheromones that instruct their behavior. With smoke in the air, guard bees cannot trip the alarm by issuing a telltale defense pheromone,[1] which allows the beekeeper to work the bees without conjuring a collective defensive response.

Modern smokers all follow the same basic design consisting of four parts: chamber, funnel lid, bellows and bellows vent. The chamber, typically cylindrical, is home to the actual fire. The funnel lid is connected to the chamber by a hinge, and is used to channel the smoke to targeted areas. The bellows, when squeezed or "puffed," generates a gust of air through the bellows vent into the chamber, where it feeds the fire with oxygen and pours smoke through the funnel lid.

Lighting a smoker is no different than lighting any kind of fire; the primary concerns are to keep it going as long as needed and produce the desired temperature and amount of smoke. You

---

1   The defense pheromone smells like banana candy, which is why many beekeepers will avoid eating bananas by their hives.

Shredded paper and plant materials make a great fire starter for the smoker.

can use any dry, organic material in your smoker; dry leaves and sticks typically work really well, and mixing in some green plant material creates additional smokiness. A small amount of shredded junk mail mixed in with the organic material is a great way to get the fire started. Many beekeepers swear by burlap for fuel as it's easy to ignite and burns slowly, but others argue that chemical residues on the fibers produce an undesirable smoke that smells bad and potentially harms the bees. If you have access, one of the best smoker fuels available, as gross as it may sound, is composted horse or cow manure.

It produces a cool, thick smoke, burns very slowly and doesn't smell bad at all.

"Oh. It's just horse manure. Horse manure's not that bad. I don't even mind the word 'manure.' You know, it's 'nure,' which is good, and a 'ma' in front of it. Ma-nure. When you consider the other choices, 'manure' is actually quite refreshing."

—George Costanza, *Seinfeld,* Episode 93: "The Soup"

You can basically use anything that burns in a pinch, but given the choice, an organic material that produces a cool, dense smoke that doesn't singe the eyes and nostrils is highly preferred.

When using your smoker it is important to give the fire time to cool down so flames are not shooting through the funnel lid every time you puff the bellows. When using a smoker beekeepers have to be hypervigilant not to cause a fire with an errant ember. It pays to be prepared and carry a fire extinguisher just in case. Start by smoking the entrance of the hive, and give it a minute or two before cracking open the lid. In most cases just a few puffs of smoke peppered throughout the inspection will achieve the desired behavior in bees. The best description of how to use smoke came to me by way of HoneyLover Susan Rudnicki, an urban beekeeper and mentor in Manhattan Beach, California. She describes using smoke as a way to "herd" her bees from harm's way. A few puffs of smoke and the bees will move away from the area, allowing you to get your fingers around a frame or replace the top board without crushing bees.

There is some debate within the treatment-free beekeeping community on whether you should smoke bees at all. On the one hand, the argument goes, bees are reliant on the smell of the hive to communicate, and by pouring smoke into the hive you mask critical communications that help regulate the health and well-being of the hive. For example, the hive might not detect unique chemical signatures of diseases thus delaying actions to remedy the situation until it is too late. On the other hand, beekeepers point to thousands of years of using smoke to great effect, and argue that not using smoke risks creating a dangerous situation, especially for those of us who keep bees in densely populated areas where angry bees can mean big trouble with neighbors. While some beekeepers with ultra-docile bees report success working without smoke, it is a practice most would characterize as unnecessarily risky. Using smoke properly has, in our research, had no measurable effect on the hive.

For thousands of years, beekeepers have used smoke while inspecting hives. (Left)

HIVE TOOLS

After having sufficiently smoked your hive and allowing a few minutes go by to let it register with the colony, the next thing on the agenda is cracking open the top board to begin the inspection. The bees have likely glued the top board on with ultra-sticky propolis, so in order to pry the top board from the hive's top box you will need to use your hive tool. The hive tool is a hand-held pry bar that comes in two basic designs, one with a hook-like feature opposite the prying end, and another with an end better suited for scraping. The design with the hook is helpful with Langstroth hives, particularly because it allows you to lift the frame out of the hive box. It can be a challenge to get the leverage needed to unstick the frame and lift it with fingers alone. The hive tool is used for dozens of beekeeping purposes, from routine inspections and adding boxes to harvesting honey and making splits. The hive tool becomes an almost unconscious extension of the beekeeper's hand, aiding in virtually every movement and action. The only problem with hive tools is finding where you last set them down. Why do they always seem to disappear?!

TRICKS OF THE TRADE AKA "HONEY HACKING"

When budgeting out the purchases necessary to get started, honey harvesting and bottling equipment should be the lowest priority, as it is entirely likely you won't need them until the second year. Should you need it in your first year and have to scramble to put it together, that is what we call a good problem. An exciting aspect of beekeeping is the fact that with a little creativity, you can make do without having the full beekeeping catalog on hand and figure out ways to whittle down your expenses. Beekeepers are tinkerers, the hackers of the insect world, constantly in search of better, more effective, less expensive and healthier ways of solving problems. Creative problem solving is a huge part of beekeeping, as is putting to use a diverse compilation of skill sets. Beekeepers are observers, theorists and behaviorists as much as they are woodworkers and agricultural laborers.

A hive tool like this makes it easier to remove the top board from a hive box. (Right)

To be resourceful and ingenious enough to solve any of the issues that pop up in beekeeping, it pays to have a few key items on hand. The first and most obvious is duct tape, the uses of which are seemingly endless. Hardware cloth is another versatile material that comes in handy for various beekeeping tasks like preparing a hive to be moved. Staple guns are handy when you need something to stay put and duct tape won't do the trick. Rubber bands are helpful any time combs need to be reattached to frames, especially when doing "cutouts"[1] of bees from a structure into hive boxes. A butcher knife is extremely helpful for any scenario requiring the cutting of honeycomb. In foundationless beekeeping, if combs are constructed across multiple frames—cross-comb—it is possible to cut them, gently straighten them and hold them in place with rubber bands (see "Fixing Cross Comb," p. 97).

Having a couple ways to make fire in your kit is generally advisable—every beekeeper at one point has gone all the way to their farthest bee yard before realizing they forgot their lighter or matches. Handheld propane or butane torches are a great way to get smokers lit quickly and can be really helpful on windy days. Some beekeepers carry a magnifying glass with them to see tiny eggs at the bottom of a cell. Confirming the presence of an egg-laying queen (see Chapter 5–Bee Sucess: How to Inspect Your Bees, Fix Common Problems and Set Up Your Hive for Prosperity, p. 89) is a top priority when inspecting any hive, and locating fresh eggs is the easiest way to do so. Additionally, in case you show up at the bee yard without a lighter or matches, magnifying glasses can easily get a fire going in your smoker.

PATIENCE

As a first-year beekeeper, your mission is to keep your bees alive while studying and observing their behavior as closely as possible. The hardest part of the first year is having patience and not sacrificing your colony's health to satisfy your sweet tooth. As legendary backwards beekeeper Kirkobeeo observes, newbees suffer from a major case of "dia*bee*tes." As is already evident, puns are an occupational hazard for beekeepers. After all new beekeepers have set up their hive, we encourage them to buy some raw honey from the beekeepers in their community to tide themselves over until their own honey can be safely harvested. Newbees can also try volunteering to help with a bee removal in exchange for a portion of the removed honey and the opportunity to learn some valuable skills.

---

1   Cutouts refer to beehive removals that involve physically cutting combs out to remove the hive.

Bees make beeswax to cap cells full of honey. (Left)

CHAPTER 3

Acquiring Honeybees Is Simple

The intense anticipation that commonly precedes acquiring honeybees, whether for the first or five hundredth time, can be all consuming. Beekeepers in much of the world have all winter to ruminate about their bees, eager for spring to thaw the earth and restart the beekeeping year. Fortunately, there is plenty to do in preparation for spring to keep beekeepers just busy and entertained enough to not drive our partners completely crazy with all manner of bee talk.

CHOOSING A LOCATION

Before the bees arrive, beekeepers should choose where their bees will reside and prepare the spot for their arrival. Hives should be positioned with consideration for one's neighbors and away from where they may be subject to vandalism, mischief and theft. Avoid placing hives in close proximity to any confined animals who could not flee if stung, such as dogs in kennels and gated backyards, chickens in confined runs or horses in stables and corrals.

Providing a relatively level surface for the hive to sit on is also critical.[1] Beekeepers can construct hive stands to compensate for uneven ground, which can also help with ant control. In areas with large numbers of ants, beekeepers can set the legs of their stands in cat food cans filled with vegetable oil as a way of creating a moat to keep the ants from climbing the stand. Alternatively, many beekeepers swear by a natural insect barrier product made from castor oil, carnauba wax and natural gum resins called Tanglefoot. The best defense for ants is the same as with all hive pests: keeping a healthy, robust hive to chase, corral, chew or carry them away.

It goes without saying that beekeepers who are prepared with their equipment, choose the spot for their hive and set it up appropriately ahead of time have a much easier time installing a new colony when the bees finally arrive. For more on selecting a location in an urban and suburban setting, check out Chapter Ten–Urban Beekeeping Basics for Tiny and Giant Backyards.

---

1   Keeping hives level will help encourage bees to draw straight comb.

WHERE TO GET YOUR BEES

Getting honeybees is the easy part, and the acquisition process is a great way to get started using the type of resourcefulness you will need to succeed as a beekeeper. There are three primary strategies for obtaining bees, each with their own merit and drawbacks:

- *Packaged Bees – $100*
- *Nucleus Colonies – $150*
- *Swarms – Pricing varies*

Our favorite method in Los Angeles is capturing a feral swarm to install (free), but let's start with the most popular process in the United States for acquiring bees: purchasing a package.

PACKAGED BEES

Packages from queen-rearing operations contain the fundamental building blocks for starting a colony of honeybees, which include an inseminated queen and 10,000–12,000 worker bees—usually about three pounds of bees. Orders for packages to be delivered in the spring start being placed as early as the previous fall and go until the supplier is sold out. Packages arrive in small, screened boxes containing a cluster of bees festooning from one another, a small tin of feed syrup and the queen in a small queen cage, sometimes accompanied by a few nurse bees to care for and feed her in transit. The bees have enough resources to survive the shipment, but should be installed as soon as weather permits.

Installing a package sounds a lot more complicated than it really is and new beekeepers can rest assured that the bees are in such a delicate state that they could hardly mount much of a defense. Still, precaution is advised and new beekeepers are encouraged to wear their suits and keep their smoker handy. Place the bottom board and bottom box where the hive will reside, then put five frames into the bottom box.

Once this hiveware is set up and ready to go, you can begin the process by positioning the package near your hive. Next, open the lid to the package and slowly remove the queen cage. Gently shake the excess bees off the cage into the bottom box. The queen is trapped in her cage by a piece of sugar candy. Use a toothpick or small twig to carefully nudge the candy loose at the entrance of the cage to enable the queen to eventually chew her way out. Place the cage with the queen inside firmly between two frames. Some beekeepers will release her directly into the hive, but are careful to ensure she doesn't fly away in the process. Next, carefully shake the remaining bees from the package into your hive in a motion Michael Bush compares to

"pour[ing] thick oil or like getting a pick out of a guitar."[1] Bees will be crawling all over the boxes, so take it slow in replacing frames and reassembling the hiveware. Don't worry, the bees will not abandon their queen and will regroup within minutes. If they are on the outside of the box, they will eventually be led inside by the queen's powerful pheromones.

Ask ten beekeepers when the best time to install your package is and you'll get twelve different answers. Ideally packages would be installed on a warm spring afternoon just before life starts slowing down for the evening. The argument for this approach holds that by installing them later in the day, you decrease the likelihood of them absconding by giving them less time to disapprove of their new home before they have to settle in for the night. If you can get them to settle for a full night, it is very likely that they will stick around.

There are numerous reasons in favor of purchasing a package, from convenience to the comfort of knowing your bees' genetics and what behavior you can expect. Beekeepers should be selective in who they choose to purchase bees from, as the bees should be suited to your particular climate. Treatment-free beekeepers may struggle to keep alive any variety of bees that haven't been specifically selected for hygienic, varroa-resistant behavior.

1   www.bushfarms.com/beespackages.htm

The priority for most queen-rearing operations in the United States has been selecting for two main traits, docility and honey production. As a result, most of the bees available for purchase and in commercial operations are lovely to work with in terms of their behavior and their honey production. However, these same bees don't possess the traits necessary to fend off the dreaded varroa mite. As mentioned, chemical treatments keep bees in a sort of suspended animation, putting off the evolution of these varroa-resistant traits. When looking for a package, ask others who have successfully kept bees without treatments. You should also get recommendations from fellow community members and ask the supplier lots of questions about their bees.

Questions to ask include:

1. Are these bees suited for my local climate?

2. Are the bees selected for durability and survival without mite treatments?

3. What kind of behavior can I expect from my bees?

The paradox in beekeeping is that often the most durable, vigorous and prolific bees can also be the most challenging to work with and have the worst attitude problems. You can probably think of a few humans who fit this description as well.

NUCLEUS COLONIES

Beekeepers can also acquire bees by purchasing what is called a "nuc" or nucleus colony from an established beekeeper. Nucs are a small colony of bees with an egg-laying queen on five deep frames, three of which should be packed with bees and brood and the other two with honey and pollen. This approach reduces the likelihood of new bees absconding and increases the chances of producing honey in the first year.

There are pros and cons to this choice. Buying a nuc from an established beekeeper generally means that you'll know the bees' genetics or at least that they have a history of workability. As with purchasing packages, when shopping for nucs you want to know about the bees you will be keeping. If the bees have a history of being treated, it may be hard to break them of that cycle in one generation. Additionally, the combs will have been contaminated by previous treatments and will need to be cycled out of the hive as soon as possible and replaced with fresh comb.

The best way to find a beekeeper who will sell you a nuc is to join a local beekeeping club, association or nonprofit and introduce yourself to the beekeepers who attend the meetings.

You can identify a queen bee among workers as the one that is the largest and longest. (Right)

Finding beekeepers who align with your beekeeping philosophy may be a tad more challenging, but keep an open mind and remember that there isn't one "right" way to keep bees that works for everyone. Learn from everyone, but think for yourself. For a small fee the beekeeper may also be willing to help install the nuc into your hive with you.

Installing a nuc sounds complicated, but is relatively straightforward. Nucs typically come in specialized boxes big enough to house five frames temporarily until they can be transferred into a regular 10-frame hive box. The bees will be closed off inside the nuc box so they can be moved to the new location. The installation process starts by smoking the nuc box and giving the bees a few minutes to settle down. Once the bees have been smoked, you can open the nuc box and begin transferring the frames one by one until all five are in the new hive box. Place the frames at the center of the hive box, and then place five empty frames to either side (two on one side, three on the other). The frames with your bees should be in the middle so the hive can expand in both directions.

Once all the frames are in and lined up, you can shake the remaining bees from the nuc box onto the top of the frames. You may have to give the bottom of the nuc box a proper drumming to get the stragglers out and into their new, more spacious home. Next use a few small puffs of smoke to encourage the bees to move off the top bars and down onto the combs, so that you can place the top board on to close it up without crushing a bunch of bees in the process. There isn't a massive rush to get the nuc installed once you start, so be calm and take your time getting them set up in their new home.

SWARMS

My favorite method of acquiring honeybees is catching a swarm. Swarms are honeybees' mode of reproduction, and while to the untrained eye they look rather menacing, swarms are generally docile and preoccupied. Honeybees establish new colonies when the existing queen bee leaves the former colony with about 60 percent of the worker bees in search of a new cavity space to colonize. Swarms consist of thousands to tens of thousands of worker bees, a few hundred drones and usually one queen. Without brood and food stores to protect, swarming bees are singularly focused on finding a new home and getting the queen there in one piece. Also, since the bees will need to build wax combs in their new home, the swarm consists of many very young bees who are still at the phase of their development when they can produce wax but haven't ventured outside the hive yet. These bees haven't matured to the point where they are able to pack much of a punch and are not all that great at flying. This contributes to the overall non-aggressive character of typical swarms. The sight of a swarm can be quite overwhelming, but the truth is that it's just a group of daughters trying not to lose their mom in the move.

Swarms of honeybees are sometimes found hanging from a branch. (Left)

Dr. Thomas Seeley has conducted extensive research aimed at discovering how swarms make decisions, from debating the merits of various nesting locations and balancing competing interests, to forming consensus and taking action. Seeley argues these decisions are reached somewhat democratically, and that bees evolved this complex behavior to process huge amounts of information and make decisions as a group. Seeley compares the individual actors in a swarm to individual neurons of primates' brains, contributing information to the decision making process in similar fashion. Even though it is composed of tens of thousands of bees, the swarm is actually a single superorganism capable of making consensus "hive-mind" decisions.

Swarming happens from spring to early summer and is commonly the result of overcrowding in the brood nest or because the hive senses it is capable of successfully reproducing itself. When the hive has made the decision to swarm, worker bees will create specialized cells called queen cells or swarm cells, which accommodate the developing queen's larger body. As the hive approaches swarming, the queen lays eggs in these queen cells where they will receive the special attention needed to grow into a queen. Larvae in queen cells are fed nutrient-dense royal jelly throughout their development and ultimately throughout their lives. This allows the queen to develop into sexual maturity, and fuels her near-constant egg laying. A virgin queen will emerge from the queen cell and after a mating flight will become the existing colony's new laying queen. In the event there are multiple virgin queens, they will battle it out with their retractable stingers until only one remains.[1]

In order for the queen bee to take flight with the swarm and make room for the new virgin queen, the worker bees will cut off the queen's diet of royal jelly days in advance so she is svelte enough to take flight. In their quest to find a new hollow space to colonize, swarms pick an intermediate location like a branch to rest on while scout bees look for new, permanent locations. Scout bees are responsible for finding a secure hollow space to establish the new colony. Swarms decide on their final location based on feedback from scout bees that report to the group using a dance similar to the waggle dance.[2] The swarm's decision is based on how excitedly and convincingly the scout bees dance. Scout bees are looking for a site that has enough volume, is protected from the elements, receives warmth from the sun, has an entrance small enough that they can defend from predators and is not infested with ants.

2   First discovered by Austrian ethologist and Nobel laureate Karl von Frisch, the figure eight–looking waggle dance is a method the honeybees use to communicate direction and distance.

1   Queens are the only honeybee in the hive that can sting multiple times without dying (and drones cannot sting at all).

Capped queen cell and queen cup. (Right)

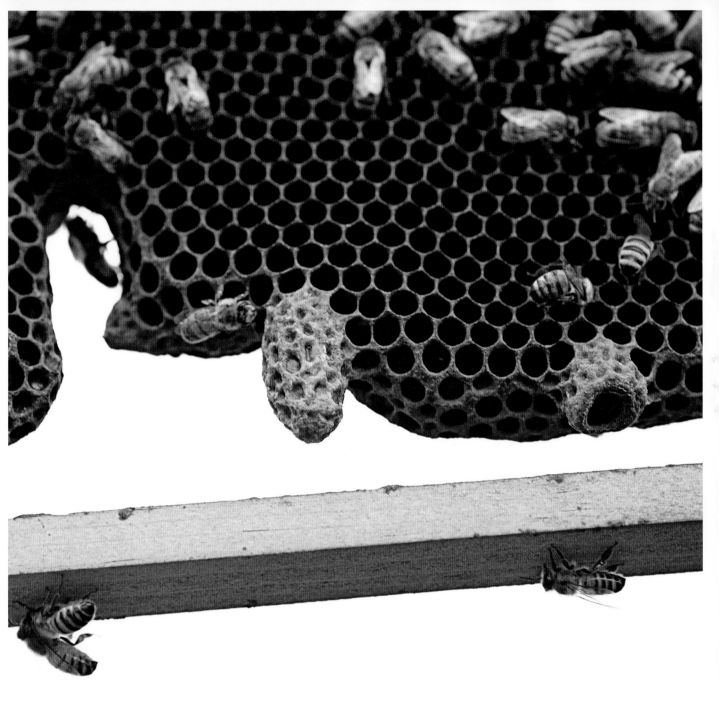

HOW TO CATCH A SWARM

Catching a swarm is one of the most enjoyable experiences in beekeeping, and is a skill which will definitely come in handy. Helping out neighbors and community members when a swarm shows up in backyards and public spaces is a great way for beekeepers to foster goodwill for bees and beekeeping. Aside from getting to play hero for people in these situations, astonished onlookers will regard beekeepers as possessing an almost magical ability to communicate with the bees. The truth is that with a basic understanding of bee behavior and the right preparations, catching a swarm is quite easy. Consistent with many aspects of beekeeping, when catching a swarm, bees do almost all the hard work.

The best time to catch a swarm is while they are resting at the intermediate location while scout bees search for new nesting sites. Most commonly swarms can be found hanging from branches of trees or bushes in a cluster, festooning from one another in a large, shape-shifting mass. To catch the swarm, you place empty hive setups, a nuc box or cardboard box with a small entrance cut out under the cluster and then clip or shake the branch so the swarm will fall into the box all at once. Ideally, the queen will drop into the box[1] along with the workers. Once the queen is in the box, the remaining workers will follow suit.

---

1   The queen bee is typically found in the center of the swarm mass.

Sam Comfort of Anarchy Apiaries, a treatment-free beekeeper and queen rearer with over 500 hives in bee yards from Vermont to South Florida, had some great advice for new beekeepers in a interview I shot for HoneyLove's YouTube Channel while attending a treatment-free conference in Oregon:

"Really you can just build a bait box, you can hang up an empty box in a tree or deer stand or out on a barn somewhere and the bees might just show up. They might choose you; it's like fishing; you don't know if it's going to work but the bees you'll find out in your area, in your environment that have survived and are swarming, are the best bees you can find. You can't buy bees like that, they are real bees."

After knocking the swarm into the box, carefully close the lid and wait for the remainder of the bees to find their way inside. If using a cardboard box or fashioning your own swarm box, be sure you leave an entrance open so everyone can rejoin the swarm. Workers will stand at the entrance of the box with their hind ends in the air fanning Nasonov, or orientation, pheromone into the air to signal the queen's new location. Beekeepers can either wait for the majority of the bees to make it inside before closing up the entrance for transport, or they can wait until after sunset when every last bee from the swarm will have made it inside the box. The fundamentals of catching a swarm are universal, but every situation will require differing levels of finesse depending on where they decide to land.

Accessibility and safety are the main concerns when capturing a swarm: Do you need a ladder? Do you need clearance from a resident or business to get access? Is it a high-traffic area on public land? These are all important things to consider before starting your rescue mission, and as with most things, it is easier when you have a beekeeping friend to assist you.

For more information check out the "How to Capture a Swarm of Honeybees" video at YouTube.com/HoneyLove.

SWARM BOXES

After a beekeeper has an established hive in their apiary, they will do just about everything they can to prevent their hive from swarming (leaving) off the property. In the event that the hive does swarm, beekeepers are advised to set out preemptive swarm boxes around the beeyard in trees and bushes where they can be placed five or six feet off the ground. You can place the boxes strategically within the swarm's likely trajectories from the hive. Swarm boxes lure their intended target by appealing to scout bees' sense of smell and their preference for cavity spaces with at least 30 to 40 liters of volume—at least one cubic foot of volume. The idea is to provide the exact real estate househunter bees are looking for during a swarm.

Beekeepers typically buy or build 5-frame nuc boxes for use as swarm boxes. Painting the frames and starter strips with beeswax helps to make the swarm box smell like home to scout bees. To mimic the Nasonov pheromone bees use to attract and orient swarms to the new location, you can use organic lemongrass oil to make the swarm box seem even more appealing. A few drops on a small piece of paper towel placed on top of the frames is enough to make the swarm box smell like that soap store at the mall. Once the swarm boxes

Bees fan Nasonov pheromone at a hive's entrance to alert other bees of the queen's location.

are sufficiently aromatic and strategically placed, monitor for activity until a swarm moves in. You can then transfer it into a proper hive box. It's a good idea to leave swarm boxes out all year, but you are most likely to find new occupants in the spring when the majority of swarming takes place. Beyond catching swarms from your own bees, swarm boxes are a great way to acquire feral bees.

If a hive is about to swarm, place swarm boxes nearby in places the bees are likely to find, like in a tree. (Left)

FERAL BEES

Feral honeybees have always been valued as a source for beekeepers to get bees that have been successful living in the local environment. Since the addition of Africanized bees, beekeepers have commonly come to look at swarms of unknown origin with suspicion. Beekeepers in regions not blessed with a climate suitable for Africanized bees can grab

swarms with little worry of getting problematic bees. However, non-Africanized bees can be every bit as fierce, so it always pays to be cautious and evaluate each swarm individually. An increasing number of beekeepers in Africanized states have taken the leap of faith with swarms, and have found the bees to be far from the vicious killers sensationalized in the news. In fact, many are now openly championing their Africanized bees and advocating for a renewed discussion on the matter. Africanized bees have been reported in the following states: California, Texas, Arizona, Nevada, New Mexico, Florida, Louisiana, Arkansas, Utah, Georgia and Tennessee. (See "Mite Resistance and the Africanized Bee," p. 104.)

If choosing to take the swarm approach of bee acquisition, it is doubly important to exercise the highest levels of caution. These better, more robust bees require better, more highly trained and experienced beekeepers who take their responsibility and the safety of others seriously. Getting lots of hands-on experience with knowledgeable beekeepers is really important, especially if you're considering using bees of unknown genetics. If new to beekeeping, it's safest to handle a feral swarm with the help of a local mentor and on-going education.

Acquiring bees is the easiest part; understanding them takes a little more effort. To understand how to be an effective beekeeper, one must have a solid grasp of honeybee biology, behavior and social organization. Knowing the life cycle of honeybees and identifying eggs, larvae and pupae is critical to assessing the health of a colony and every other aspect of beekeeping. With this understanding, beekeepers can set up their bees for success by encouraging their natural tendencies.

Feral bees moving into a swarm box. (Left)

CHAPTER 4

Getting to Know Your Superorganisms

THE BUSY BEE

Honeybees are synonymous with hard work; humans have always marveled at their fastidious work ethic. We have long admired their productivity, selflessness and willingness to sacrifice themselves on behalf of their community. Honeybees are alchemists and brew masters, able to transform nectar into sweet, golden honey. Worker bees at the foraging phase of their lives engage in a turbocharged pursuit of nectar until they literally work their wings off. Once a worker bee cannot fly any longer, she is of no further use to the colony and is unceremoniously left to die outside the hive.

The bees' lifelong quest for nectar unwittingly results in the sexual reproduction of countless plant species through pollination. As bees crawl into each blossom to drink nectar with their complex mouthparts, the branched hairs that cover their body brush against the blossom's anther and become covered in pollen. This pollen contains the plant's gametes or sperm cells, so when the honeybee flies to the next blossom, she transfers the pollen to the new blossom's stigma. Pollination transfers genes among members of a plant species, ensuring the production of seeds and producing the next generation of the plant.

Scientists theorize that plants and bees began co-evolving over the past hundred million years when plants began to reproduce through flowers that captured wind-blown pollen. Human diets have always indirectly relied on pollinators, and since the adoption of agriculture, humans have become increasingly reliant on bees to produce our staple foods. Without bees pollinating our food crops, we would not only have a very mundane diet, but the simple act of feeding ourselves would be a challenge. Without pollinators it would be exceedingly difficult to produce some of our favorite foods: almonds, oranges, strawberries, onions, cashews, beets, papaya, watermelon, soybeans, apples, cherries, grapes, cocoa and at least 80 other food crops. To feed the ever-growing human population of the future, we must take action now to protect our pollinators and create food systems that place a higher value on their services. Food systems of the future will have to be more sustainable through efficiency, localization and new ways of dealing with pests that do not rely on potentially destructive chemicals.

SUPERORGANISMS

Probably the most mind-boggling aspect of honeybees is the fact that they are a "superorganism." No, that doesn't mean that they have alter egos and fight crime under the cover of darkness. And while they are definitely the superheroes of the insect world, honeybees are called superorganisms because the *colony*, and not the individual bee, is the basic unit of measurement for the species. The individual honeybee cannot survive on her own, and especially *his* own, outside the context of the colony. The colony is the sum of all of its parts—queen, workers, drones, brood, combs, propolis and all manner of microorganisms—which add up to a single organism.

Honeybee society is characterized as "eusocial," which means they live in groups and divide up the work of foraging for food, caring for young, constructing the nest and defending the colony. A honeybee seen buzzing from flower to flower is only able to do so because she is a member of the colony. The collective efforts of tens of thousands of related honeybees is what allows the hive to function. The many roles honeybees play throughout their lives allow the hive to operate like an individual mammal. The combs act as the flesh and bones; the queen acts as the reproductive organs; the brood nest is the womb; forager bees are like the arms and legs used to gather food; the guard bees are like claws or fangs for self-defense; nurse bees secrete royal jelly through specialized glands to feed young larvae like a mother producing milk. The combined bee behaviors produce results similar to the cognitive functions and immune systems of mammals.

As a superorganism comprised of tens of thousands of individuals, honeybees have developed highly complex forms of communication that allow the hive-mind to make consensus decisions about what to forage, when to defend the hive and where to swarm. Honeybee communication is primarily facilitated through pheromones—glandular secretions that transmit messages and elicit certain behavioral responses from members of the colony. Pheromones, for example, are used to signal alarm and alert guard bees to defend the hive. Alarm pheromones are released when a guard bee stings the intruder, and the barbed stinger left behind continues to emit the banana-scented chemical into the air to help more guard bees zero in on the offender's location for another round of stings.

Pheromones are also critical to brood rearing by helping nurse bees recognize and care for brood at the various stages of larval growth. Bees use pheromones to coordinate countless physiological functions of the hive, many likely unknown to us, from helping drones mate with queens to inhibiting the growth of ovaries in the colony's worker bees.

Sounds and vibrations also likely play a massive role in honeybee communication, from the piping sounds virgin queens make like a battle cry once they've hatched to help

Barbed stinger after being stung

determine which queen will inherit the hive, to the noticeable change in tone of the hive's buzzing in response to smoke. Most of a honeybee's life is spent in the darkness of the hive, which means they must rely on all of their senses to communicate and interpret complex data.

Honeybees also communicate through the waggle dance, a series of high-energy movements foragers use to recruit others to productive food sources. This figure-eight dance move was first decoded by Nobel laureate Karl von Frisch, who determined that it signaled to other foragers the distance, direction and quality of sources of pollen and nectar. The directions to the food source are coded in the size and angle of the figure-eight shaped movements, and the quality of the forage is communicated by how enthusiastically she waggles and how rapidly she dances around. The more dramatic her performance is, the more workers she will recruit to her foraging location. The waggle dance also likely shares the smell of the nectar among fellow foragers to help them navigate to the food source by following their noses.

Nurse bees on capped brood

BEE MATH

Honeybees are insects descended from predatory wasps, and have been around for approximately 72 million years. Bees follow the basic insect blueprint with a few specialized modifications. Bees have three distinct body parts—head, thorax and abdomen—with four wings, six legs and five eyes, two of which are compound and three of which are small ocelli eyes, two antennae and an exoskeleton made mostly of chitin. All honeybees begin life as a tiny, white, rice-shaped egg laid by a queen bee at the bottom of a wax cell. Three days after it's laid, the egg hatches into a larva, a phase of development where the brood resembles a tiny, worm-like creature curled up at the bottom of a cell. Nurse bees feed royal jelly, a nutrient-dense secretion, to the larva for two days and then switch to brood food, fermented pollen, until pupation starts on the sixth day.

The larva pupates in the cell and creates a cocoon, which produces a cap on the cell. Once the pupa has capped the cell and becomes "capped brood," it begins the metamorphosis process that transforms the worm-like creature into a bee. On the twenty-first day, the bee chews its way out of the cell and her life of service begins almost immediately. This process happens like clockwork; the entire process takes exactly 21 days for workers, 24 days for drones and 15 to 16 days for queens. Beekeepers call this "bee math," and memorizing it allows you to better read the hive and evaluate the queen.

Nurse bees on open brood (Right)

QUEEN BEE

Historically, humans have looked at the hive as a model of perfected social order, and have at various times used it to justify everything from caste systems and slavery to monarch rule and religious piety. All of these attempts, of course, were disastrously ill-fated as human and honeybee social order bear absolutely no resemblance to each other whatsoever. Still we must use the language we have to describe the world we are observing. Even though we know bee society is nothing like a monarchy, we continue to describe queen bees as such for their seeming absolute rule over the hive. There is no human analogue for a queen bee's actual role in the hive, but we have a hard time describing her as anything but a queen because she seems to be the highest-ranking member of the hive.

As the only sexually developed female in the hive, the queen's primary responsibility is egg laying. A queen is distinguished from an ordinary worker bee based on her diet and the specialized cell where she pupates. During larval development, queens are fed a bulk diet of royal jelly, a nutritious secretion young bees produce from hypopharyngeal glands and feed to developing brood. Queen bees get a buffet-size portion as they develop in specialized cells called queen cells. This diet allows queens to develop ovaries, and the queen cell's size and shape accommodate the growth of her much larger abdomen. In addition to hosting the queen's reproductive organs, her enlarged abdomen and a specialized organ called an ovipositor uniquely allows her to deposit eggs at the bottom of each wax cell. At peak production, a queen can lay upwards of 1,500 eggs per day!

Queens themselves transform from egg to larva to bee in just fifteen to sixteen days. A week after emerging from her cell, a virgin queen goes on mating flights to visit drone congregation areas. Drones, who play no role in food production, primarily function as the hive's way of sharing their genes with virgin queens of other colonies. In preparation for this momentous event, drones congregate together outside the hive with fellow drones from other hives to wait for a suitor-seeking, virgin queen to fly on by. Everyone loves to compare this aspect of bee biology to human males, with drone congregation areas akin to pubs where amorous males join forces in search of females with matching carnal desires. Women tend to enjoy that comparison a great deal more than their male counterparts. The story gets all the richer when you add the fact that drones ultimately perish as a result of copulation, their everted endophallus—penis—and attached abdominal tissues are forcefully ripped off upon insemination.

Virgin queens take mating flights over a couple of days, mating with a dozen or so drones. Drones will remove what remains of the former suitor drone in order to follow suit. Inseminated queens return to the hive where worker bees remove the last lucky drone's penis, which signals to the colony that she is mated and everything is right with the world. The number of times a queen mates is a factor in determining how attractive she is to the worker bees and whether they will accept her or replace her at first chance.

Workers surround a queen bee. (Left)

Promiscuity seems to be rewarded in honeybee queens. The greater the number of drones the queen mates with, the greater the potential for genetic diversity within the hive. Beekeepers of feral bees notice tremendous variation in the size and color of their bees, and attribute their bees vigor to this diversity. The queen stores the semen from her mating flights for the remainder of her life, and will use it to lay eggs until the colony's workers feel her productivity is inadequate, or she becomes injured, in which case they will initiate a swarm sequence or raise a new queen.

Approximately 48 hours after returning to the hive from her last mating flight, the queen starts laying eggs, and the colony becomes what beekeepers call "queen right."

Worker bees are sterile females that care for the hive.

WORKER BEES

There is an ebb and flow in the availability of honeybees' forage, and fertile queens lay eggs in corresponding numbers. When there is a nectar flow queens are raising an army of worker bees to capture as much of the available resources as possible. As the flow tapers off and approaches the seasonal dearth, the number of eggs she lays slows way down.

Worker bees are sterile females who do virtually all of the work in and out of the hive. From the moment of their birth, worker bees begin a progression of age-related jobs beginning within the hive and culminating as foragers out gathering pollen, nectar, propolis and water. For over half of their short lives, workers toil within the hive building wax combs, caring for the queen, nursing and feeding brood, regulating the temperature of the hive, cleaning up refuse, picking off parasites, taking out the sick and dead and, of course, guarding the hive's entrance.

NURSE BEES

After a worker emerges from her cell, she is fed and cared for by slightly older nurse bees. She almost immediately goes to work cleaning and preparing her cell for its next occupant. By day three worker bees progress to the nurse bee phase of their lives. Their main responsibility is to feed royal jelly and brood food, also referred to as beebread, to larvae until day eleven when their hypopharyngeal gland responsible for producing the nutritious secretion atrophies. Once workers lose the ability to create royal jelly, another equally amazing ability comes online: wax secretion.

Nurse bees care for brood by feeding them royal jelly and beebread. (Right)

House bees store colorful pollen that will later be made into beebread.

HOUSE BEES

For the next five or six days, workers become wax or house bees as a result of their ability to secrete wax from glands located between segments of their abdomens. This phase is spent building new wax combs, repairing old cells, capping honey cells and aiding in food storage by receiving pollen and nectar from forager bees. House bees receive forager bees returning with pollen in their pollen baskets, and begin the process of transforming the raw pollen into an edible product. Brood food or "beebread" is a mixture of a hypopharyngeal component,

saliva, pollen and nectar. Worker bees ram this combo into cells for storage with the tops of their heads, and in so doing inoculate it with specialized microbes that aid in fermentation. Recent studies have shown that there are over 188 species of fungi and 29 kinds of bacteria that contribute to the fermentation of pollen into beebread. One can easily extrapolate how disruptive fungicides and antibiotics can be to a colony that depends on both fungi and bacteria to produce its staple food.

Bees take orientation flights to orient themselves around the hive.

FLIGHT SCHOOL

Twenty-one days after hatching, house bees begin daily orientation flights to learn the location of their hive and earn their wings, so to speak. These orientation flights are often mistaken for swarming by new beekeepers because at times it can look like thousands of bees flying excitedly around the hive. Since queens can lay over one thousand eggs a day, there is the potential for thousands of bees to go through "flight school" on the same day. Bees venturing outside of the hive for the first time in their lives take these orientation flights to familiarize themselves with their surroundings. Bees launch themselves into the air and begin flying back and forth in front of the hive in arcs which increase in length until they have orbited, scanned and memorized their home for several minutes, at which point they return to the hive.

These practice runs for later foraging missions allow bees to orient themselves in relation to the sun and visual patterns in their habitat, which will help them to navigate their environment. Going with the flight school metaphor, you can think of this as calibrating their GPS to their home coordinates so they can go exploring for nectar and always find their way home. Bees continue this daily ritual until they advance to the foraging stage and begin taking numerous daily foraging flights. They will continue to forage for the essentials—nectar, pollen, water and plant resins, or propolis, until their wings wear out and they die. A worker's life span ranges depending on what time of year she emerges from her cell. Workers born in the foraging season will wear out their wings and die in as little as six weeks, whereas workers born in the fall may live as long as six months so they can help kickstart the colony the following spring.

DRONES

Drones are male honeybees, and as the most disparaged member of bee society, they are probably the actors whose role in the hive we understand the least. Humans have thought up all kinds of ways to explain the role of drones in the hive. Mostly these attempts have been mired by attribution of human-like traits, often going so far as to judge them on their moral character. Worse yet, humans have tried to compare other humans to drones, likening the drones' perceived lack of work ethic as evidence of moral and spiritual shortcomings. Drones leave all the foraging to the worker bees, and play no noticeable role in the hive's food production other than to benefit from the labor of others. You can see how dangerous trying to draw parallels to human society can be when looking to the hive for answers.

Alas, to this day we continue to describe the maligned drone in terms of human qualities. It's tempting to describe the drone as lazy moochers who just drink honey and hang out with their bros all day waiting for a sexy, young virgin queen to take flight. While there is some truth to this assessment, the drone's role in the hive is likely far more complex than we imagine.

Drones start out life just like queens and workers; however, unlike their female hivemates, drones are a result of an unfertilized egg. Drones are haploid, which means they only possess the one set of chromosomes passed on by the queen. Drone development takes 24 days versus the workers' 21-day cycle from egg to honeybee. Also in contrast to workers, stinger-less drones do not follow the same progression of age-related jobs.

Drones' contributions to the hive are far less obvious or apparent, but their presence is beneficial to the colony. Drones are reported to contribute to the morale of the hive; beekeepers anecdotally note that the presence of drones makes their bees "happy." Drones probably also contribute to temperature regulation by fanning their wings to help cool the hive, or vibrating their bodies to create warmth when needed. Their primary and undisputed job responsibility is to disseminate genetic material to other honeybee colonies, which is a fancy way of saying it's their job to have sex with virgin queens from other hives.

As bee breeding has become more and more industrialized, the insemination process for queens has become the domain of the

Worker bee (left) and drone (right)

laboratory. Breeders rely on artificial insemination to ensure genetic purity of their bees, which contrasts the "promiscuous queen" concept noted earlier as a successful strategy employed by feral bees. This reliance on artificial insemination has encouraged a sort of anti-drone culture among beekeepers who look at them as dispensable.

Some beekeepers who advocate destruction of drone comb argue the practice boosts honey production, discourages swarming and helps to remove pests. The only reason to remove drone comb that bears any scrutiny is to manage mite loads in the hive. Varroa mites prefer to prey on drone brood due to their longer, 24-day pupation period. This allows the varroa mite eggs to hatch and mature in time for their host to emerge from his cell. For more on varroa mites and how to deal with them, flip to page 103.

It is easy for new beekeepers to feel overwhelmed by the amount of information there is to know about honeybees, but you aren't required to know everything before you start. In fact, most of the information and techniques are learned on the job. Beekeepers often surprise themselves with how quickly they are able to learn about bees, just by spending some time with their hands in the hive. Half of the battle is just learning the vocabulary and cutting through the jargon. The best way to get the information to stick is to join a beekeeper as they inspect their bees and pair hands-on visuals with the vocabulary and concepts. The beekeeping experience is enhanced and the learning curve shortened when beekeepers seek out mentors who can help translate what they are seeing. In the end, beekeeping should be fun, and approached as a lifelong learning opportunity.

CHAPTER 5

Bee Success: How to Inspect Your Bees, Fix Common Problems and Set Up Your Hive for Prosperity

INSPECTING YOUR HIVE

After installing a package or nuc, the next likely interaction new beekeepers will have with their bees is the first inspection. Inspections generally take less than one hour, but make sure you have a buffer of time in case you need to dive deeper into the hive. Learning how to properly inspect a hive is a critical skill for beekeepers, and over a lifetime it becomes an art form. Before beekeepers even begin to light their smokers or crack the hive open, they should visualize their actions beforehand. This allows the beekeeper to inspect bees with calm, deliberate actions and minimize the impact on the hive. Keen observational skills and contingency plans allow beekeepers to react to the various issues that may arise when hives are inspected. It also helps to have all the right gear.

The essential equipment for inspecting hives

INSPECTION EQUIPMENT CHECKLIST

- ✔ *Protective clothing*
  - ➖ *veil*
  - ➖ *suit*
  - ➖ *gloves*
  - ➖ *boots*
  - ➖ *thick socks*
- ✔ *Smoker with extra fuel: leaves, twigs, burlap, etc.*
- ✔ *Lighter or matches*
- ✔ *Hive tool*

- ✔ *Magnifying glass*
- ✔ *Sharp knife*
- ✔ *Thin rubber bands*

OPTIONAL/SEASONAL EQUIPMENT

- ✔ *Additional hive boxes and frames*
- ✔ *Clean 5-gallon bucket with lid*
- ✔ *1-gallon plastic bags*

Hive tool on top board

The primary purpose of inspecting the hive is to confirm the queen's presence and evaluate her health and productivity. You may wonder how in the world you'll find a queen amidst tens of thousands of bees, much less judge her fitness and vigor. Even if you do notice the queen, aside from injuries or deformities, you won't learn much about her health from appearances alone. Beekeepers have to read all the road signs along the way, and draw conclusions based on these findings. It helps to have a mental checklist—bonus points if you keep written records!

The first step in hive inspection is smoking the bees. Once the smoker has been lit and is producing thick plumes of smoke, release a few puffs (2–3) of smoke near the hive's entrance and return 30 seconds later for a few more. You can offer up a periodic puff over the next four or five minutes and let the smoke work its magic.

There is no reason to rush this part of the process, and you should be careful not to overdo it with the smoke. That said, don't be shy with using smoke—make sure it is getting through the entrance. It's a balancing act, but by paying careful attention to the bees' behavior, you can get a read on how much smoke is required and adjust accordingly. If they are bouncing off your veil and reacting to your breath, use more smoke; if they don't seem to be paying attention to you or bothered by your activity, dial it back a notch. You'll get a feel for it with practice.

The first thing you'll notice is a change in the tone of the hive's buzzing in reaction to the smoke. Any bees near the entrance of the hive will run inside to eat honey. You may also notice that smoke disrupts the flow of foragers returning to the hive by masking the pheromones they use to navigate their way home.

After patiently smoking the entrance, the next step is to remove the top board. Chances are the bees have glued the top board to the hive box with propolis, which means you'll have to use your hive tool to pop the top. It helps to wedge the prying end of the hive tool in and out at various points between the top board and hive box to greatly reduce the popping sound made when the two parts unstick. Sometimes frames can be stuck to the top board, so it pays to go slowly and ease the lid off with care.

Telling the difference between combs being used for baby bees in the brood nest and combs used to store honey and pollen can be difficult at first, but with experience you will soon be able to easily recognize one from the other. Take the time to actually study what is in each cell. The frame can have some of everything—open and capped brood, nectar, honey, beebread and pollen. Because of this, you'll have to carefully inspect the activity in the cells to understand the frame's utility. For example, is it a brood frame or a food frame? Honey is fairly easy to spot, from the open cells of nectar to the white-capped cells of honey. If you have used smoke, you'll notice the bees headfirst in cells drinking honey and nectar. Bees have a tendency to store their honey above the brood nest. If you are unsure, you can always use your hive tool to puncture a capped cell to see if honey runs out. Brood is of course noticeably different, but it comes in various states of larval growth and pupation. If you notice that there are little white worm-like creatures curled up at the bottom of the cell—called open brood—you know you are looking at a comb from the brood nest. If you see cells with brownish caps—capped brood—you are looking at brood that have entered their final phases of pupation and will be hatching soon.

Once the top board is cracked open, a few gentle puffs of the smoker down through the frames and into the hive can help calm any offended bees. Now the inspection really begins. Using the hive tool, gently nudge the frame with the most wiggle room free from any propolis. When you set up your hive boxes, you want to push all the frames to one side. Doing this will leave an extra quarter inch and give you enough space to lift out the first frame without disturbing the adjacent comb. If using a hive tool with a hook end, slide that end between frames to help lift it out. From there, each frame can be inspected individually. The empty space permits the beekeeper to slide the frame away from the rest so it can be lifted out of the box for inspection without crushing bees or comb. This process is repeated until the beekeeper has seen sufficient evidence of a healthy, egg-laying queen.

The first telltale sign of a queen is the presence of eggs. After installing a package or swarm, the main objective of the first inspection is to confirm the presence of eggs; where there are eggs, there are various stages of brood. You can usually observe brood of all ages within the same comb. Spotting tiny white, granular eggs at the bottom of a cell can be a challenge without the help of a magnifying glass. For some, eggs are visible to the naked eye, but for most a little magnification will make all the difference.

Eggs in wax cells (Left)

FINDING THE QUEEN

Spotting a queen amid tens of thousands of bees among dozens of combs can be a challenge at times, even if she is marked with a big red dot. Queens purchased from commercial queen-rearing operations are marked with different color paint each year so you can easily spot her and know her age. The queen is larger and a slightly different hue than workers, but she can easily blend in amid the swirl of activity on each comb. Plus, the combination of smoke and sunlight could inspire the queen to run for cover. When she wants to be, she can be quite elusive. You can narrow your search by reading behavioral cues that tip you off to her general vicinity. For starters, the queen is likely to be found in or near the brood nest, so you can start your search in the area most populated with bees. Work your way through the hive, carefully inspecting each frame and reading the bees' behavior for clues.

Workers act differently around queens, taking orders from her powerful pheromones. One dead giveaway of her general location is the tendency bees have to march directly to their queen, instinctively drawn to her presence through aromatic commands. Bees use specialized sensory receptors in their antennae and mouth to interpret the various chemical pheromones used to communicate and elicit collective behaviors. Workers are said to be calmed in the presence of their queen and will often form a circle around her like adoring fans.

Of course, smoke disrupts bees' ability to send and receive the coded messages that dictate the behaviors you're hoping to observe when searching for a queen. By using smoke sparingly and exercising patience, you are more likely to observe the behaviors that help pinpoint the queen's location. Practice will help you sharpen your observational skills and cut down the time it takes to locate the queen. Don't feel like you have to find the queen during your first inspection or any thereafter, because the less time you have the hive open, the better, and there isn't any real reason to waste time searching for her if you confirm her presence by locating fresh eggs.

Queen bee amid a flurry of activity (Right)

FIXING CROSS COMB

Foundationless beekeepers must be careful to correct combs from veering off course and becoming cross comb[1] by using a sharp knife and rubber bands to hold combs in place. Regularly inspecting your bees during the spring is important for your hive to remain inspectable. This process, if caught early on, is quite simple to correct. Simply pull out the cross-comb frames from the hive as a solid unit. Next, use your knife to separate the stray comb from the neighboring frame (cut the comb from where it is attached to the top bar) and gently bend the comb back into the alignment with the original frame. The key is to make the least mess possible when cutting the combs so the bees have less to repair after you are through. Thin rubber bands stretched vertically around the frames may then be used to hold the combs in place until the bees have a chance to reattach them to the frame. The bees will chew through the rubber bands and then drag them out of the hive.

One of Chelsea's favorite memories of our hives was watching what she called a "bee on a string." The rubber band being hauled out of the hive got stuck on a splinter of wood and the bee spent a solid minute of flying in place until it came loose.

1   Cross comb is a comb that has veered off the straight line of the frame and crosses onto the neighboring frame (or frames).

INSPECT REGULARLY AND RECORD YOUR OBSERVATIONS

Subsequent inspections require a slightly higher degree of scrutiny. You'll still evaluate the queen on the same basis, but now that the hive has had a chance to build up, you have more data to interpret for that evaluation. Taking stock of the food stores the hive has produced relative to the time of year is always an important consideration. A good rule of thumb is one frame of honey and half of pollen for every frame of brood. A well-fed 10-frame hive would have four frames of honey, two frames of pollen and four frames of brood. Perhaps more important for insight into to the queen's stability and productivity is the queen's laying pattern. Laying patterns are easiest observed in portions of comb with capped brood. You want to see solid patterns with the majority of cells put to use (see photo on page 99). Beekeepers interpret spotty patterns as potential evidence of disease or a weak queen. You have to be careful to interpret everything within the context of the time of year and the hive's history, however. If the hive has a history of not building up, spotty patterns are an indication of queen problems or pests. If the hive is otherwise a great hive, a spotty pattern may just be a result of the time of year and the natural brood cycles.

Langstroth hive with a full box of cross-comb frames (Left)

Solid laying pattern

One of the most important things you can do during an inspection is write down your observations so you and your mentor can use that data to problem solve or make decisions down the road. Having a record helps you keep track of your hives. It can often be weeks between inspections and without notes it can be hard to recall all of the details. This data helps you plan your inspection and course of action *before* you open up the hive and start moving things around. This in turn helps your bees because it reduces the amount of time their hive is open to the elements, and it prevents you from making dumb "game-time" decisions. Believe it or not, it can be a challenge to think on your feet when you have a colony of over 50,000 stinging insects open next to those feet. Like elite athletes who picture their victory going into competition, you should mentally plot out your actions before cracking open that lid and saying hello to your bees.

Foundationless frames should be maintained through regular inspection. (Left)

INSPECTING FOR DISEASE

Treatment-free beekeepers must look out for potential bee diseases and pests, perhaps to an even greater degree than conventional beekeepers. Diagnosing a hive can be challenging for any beekeeper, and to be a responsible member of the beekeeping community you should be able to recognize signs of trouble. Tomes have been written about bee diseases and what to do about them, a great deal of which is available online. Between Wikipedia, YouTube and Google image searches, beekeepers can try to solve what ails their bees. A disease like American foulbrood requires swift attention as it can spread quickly throughout an apiary, and is easily carried to nearby hives. Beekeepers must be vigilant in monitoring for signs of the bacterial disease as it is highly contagious and can spread rapidly.

AMERICAN FOULBROOD

American foulbrood is caused by a bacterium spread by spores, and is perhaps the most destructive brood disease of honeybees. The bacterium responsible for the destruction is called *Paenibacillus larvae.* This bacterium attacks larvae inside capped cells, causing a failure to pupate and turning the larvae into a brownish slime inside the cell. Beekeepers often first notice an unpleasant rotting smell and confirm their suspicions upon finding sunken, soggy and disrupted cell cappings. If brood cells appear to be affected, use a toothpick or small branch to poke inside the suspected cells. If the gunk inside the cell sticks to the toothpick and is stringy when pulled back out, the hive is almost certainly infected. Almost every state requires beekeepers to immediately burn the entire hive and carefully scorch any re-used equipment with a propane or butane hand torch to kill any lingering spores.

CHALKBROOD

Chalkbrood is a brood disease caused by a fungus called *Ascosphaera apis.* Chalkbrood progresses from cotton-like white mold during fungal growth, causing the larvae to swell inside the cell. The larvae dry out and harden into white or gray chalk-like "mummies." Worker bees will remove chalkbrood mummies from their cells and dispose of them outside of the hive.

NOSEMA

The most common disease that affects adult honeybees is Nosema, a dysentery-like condition spread by spores transmitted through infected bee feces. Nosema interferes with bees' ability to digest pollen and produce brood food. It is most abundant in hives during the winter when bees can't take cleansing flights to defecate. Nosema is confirmed through microscopic analysis and is next to impossible to diagnose with the naked eye. One visual indication of nosema is bee poop on combs along with piles of dead/dying bees. Replacing old combs with new ones is an effective way to limit the spread of spores from year to year.

It's important to regularly inspect for disease in the brood nest. (Right)

VARROA MITES

"The thing I never understood about bee people is their obsession with mites, mites, mites, mites! It makes me wonder if dog people get together and go to conferences to sit around and talk about their dog's fleas?! Can you imagine?"

–HoneyLover Kirk Anderson, urban beekeeper and mentor, in response to the question, "What do you do about mites?"

After romping their way around the globe leaving a wake of destruction in their path, varroa mites descended upon American hives in 1987, and within twenty years they had infiltrated hives in all 50 states, including Hawaii. As with many invasive species, varroa mites were swept up in the tides of globalization from their native habitat in southeast Asia and carried all over the planet. Varroa mites likely made the jump from their original host *Apis cerana* in their Southeast Asian natural habitat to imported *Apis mellifera*. From there they spread hive to hive all over the world becoming a truly global pain in the ass.

According to Kim Flottum, *Bee Culture* editor, author and conventional beekeeper, "You can link varroa mites to nearly everything that's wrong with beekeeping these days. Because they stubbornly refuse to succumb to most preventative measures or treatments, we have to learn to live with them."[1]

Varroa mites cause beekeepers such grief because they quickly proliferate and can crash a hive in short order. Pregnant mites slip past nurse bees into brood cells and lay their eggs just after the brood is capped. Young mites, typically seven to ten females and one male, hatch ten days later, right as the young bee host is emerging from its cell. This next generation of mites spreads to other bees and brood, pausing only to suck the bees' blood for sustenance and swap genetic material. Drones are the mites' preferred prey as their pupation takes two days longer than that of worker bees, giving the mite eggs longer to hatch and gain strength.

By damaging the bees' physical body and immune system, varroa mites open the floodgates for a variety of viral infections that capitalize on the hive's weakened state. If the colony's health is further compromised by stress, malnutrition or residual pesticides, the combined effects often prove lethal. There are several ways to determine the level of mites in the hive, including sugar shakes,[2] drone uncappings and the presence of mite feces inside cells. However, there are no satisfactory ways to fully get rid of them once they have been counted. As Kirkobeeo says, all mite tests do is leave you with a number and not any solutions.

2   "Sugar shakes" refers to a method of mite test where you take a sample of bees and cover them with powdered sugar to count the number of mites present.

1   *Better Beekeeping: The Ultimate Guide to Keeping Stronger Colonies and Healthier, More Productive Bees* pp. 134
Queen with varroa mites (Left)

Beekeepers who have tried to treat with chemicals refer to them as "wonder chemicals," because they wonder if they work and wonder why they cost so much. Those hardy beekeepers are the first to speak up and say that chemical treatments—whether pyrethroids, organophosphates or formic acids—simply don't work and are harmful to bees. As Kim Flottum said:

> "The use of any chemicals in vogue is a fundamental crime against our product, our livestock and our way of life."[1]

MITE RESISTANCE AND THE AFRICANIZED BEE

According to Randy Oliver, biologist, conventional migratory beekeeper, lecturer, publisher of ScientificBeekeeping.com, author of countless articles for *The American Bee Journal* and proponent of "Whatever Works For You" beekeeping:

> "There is some evidence that some lineages are innately more resistant to certain parasites.[2] The question that haunts me is to what degree our recent elevated rate of colony mortality might be due to the limited gene pool of our managed stocks, which may simply be lacking critical genes for resistance to the onslaught of our recently introduced parasites and the associated virus issues. Such a problem would likely be self-correcting if it weren't for the nearly universal reliance upon medications by our queen producers."[3]

Controlling mites is seen as the bedrock of responsible beekeeping, and developing mite-resistant bees is the only widely accepted solution. Though the majority of beekeepers continue to eye them with suspicion and derision, the highly sensationalized Africanized bees have actually emerged as a leading candidate in the search for mite-resistant bees. Beekeepers from the southern United States all the way to Brazil have fully embraced Africanized bees and adjusted their beekeeping practices accordingly, such as wearing full suits and veils and using plenty of smoke. Keepers of feral Africanized bees note very low mite mortality rates and largely attribute it to the bees' ability to detect infected brood and remove it from the hive. Their smaller size, grooming behaviors, propolis collection and variable cell size in feral colonies, are also thought to play a role in Africanized bees' durability.

Throughout the past ten years, an increasing number of American beekeepers have also begun re-evaluating Africanized bees because of their reputation for durability and the prospect of saving money on chemical treatments. These hybrid bees have won over many beekeepers due to cost savings alone. The extra time and care it takes to go through an Africanized hive should be offset by money and time not spent treating bees with expensive chemicals. Disparage the Africanized bee all you want, but it is hard to argue with cost savings.

1   *Better Beekeeping: The Ultimate Guide to Keeping Stronger Colonies and Healthier, More Productive Bees* pp. 135

2   Oxley, PR and BP Oldroyd (2009) Mitochondrial sequencing reveals five separate origins of 'black' Apis mellifera (Hymenoptera: Apidae) in eastern Australian commercial colonies. Journal of Economic Entomology 102(2):480-484.

3   http://scientificbeekeeping.com/whats-happening-to-the-bees-part-5-is-there-a-difference-between-domesticated-and-feral-bees/

While some American beekeepers have a zero tolerance policy toward Africanized bees, many will concede that they would be happy to keep them under the right circumstances—usually far from where they could pose a risk. There is some merit to the proximity concern; beekeepers should always be respectful of their neighbors and employ a safety-first approach.

Unfortunately, there are no perfect metrics for evaluating Africanized bees early in the colony's life to determine whether they will behave acceptably or if they will be deemed too fierce to keep. The hive's temperament can fluctuate throughout the year depending on the strength of the hive and resource availability. Bees that were gentle as lambs when there was work to be done during the nectar flow can turn into wolves while defending their hives during the dearth. Perhaps a better comparison is a mother bear defending her cubs. Even as huge colonies they can stay just as gentle and workable as ever. This has earned Africanized bees a reputation for being unpredictable, and gives some beekeepers pause.

Some of the most successful treatment-free beekeepers keep bees that others would consider unworkable, but they are often out in the desert and far from highly populated areas. These same bees could be quite problematic for migratory beekeepers who move their hives frequently and have to be able to quickly inspect hundreds of hives in a day. Beekeepers have to decide for themselves the degree to which they are willing to put up with naughty behavior, but no one should set themselves up for trouble by keeping highly defensive bees in unsafe locations. Some Africanized hives can be simply too fierce to work, and if possible, should be requeened immediately. It can be exceedingly difficult to locate a queen amid a hive of angry bees, and should not be attempted in close proximity to other people or pets. (See "Mean Bees—Removing a Queen," starting on p. 114.)

Africanized bees are of course not the end-all solution for mites, but they offer a glimmer of hope for the prophesied mite-resistant bees that beekeepers have been hoping for. As far as Randy Oliver sees it, "Our locally adapted 'survivor,' feral populations may be an invaluable resource for bee breeders, offering the prospect of being our salvation from the varroa-virus complex." He feels strongly that "feral survivor stocks deserve far more of our attention than we have been giving them."

Development of mite-resistant bees is the panacea to all of the challenges beekeepers must face to keep their bees healthy, their businesses afloat and their families happy. Beekeepers long for the day when varroa-related anxiety disorder is a thing of the past. In the meantime, beekeepers can throw out the practices that affect honeybees' natural behavior, reproductive cycle, diet and immune systems, and disrupt their delicate relationship with pests, parasites, pathogens and the mind-boggling microbiological diversity inhabiting thousands of ecologies unique to honeybee colonies. Beekeepers must abandon the destabilizing modern innovations created in service of efficiency, productivity and profit, the true costs of which have been paid for with the health of our honeybees. By the time we ditch all the naughty behavior, clean up our act, and start treating hives with the respect a superorganism deserves, we may find we don't need the coveted mite-resistant super bee to rescue beekeeping and discover that honeybees are up for the challenge.

DRONES AND MITES

One way to determine to what degree the hive has varroa mites is to uncap ten to twenty drone cells and count the number that are covered in tiny red parasites. If a high percentage of the larvae are infected, the beekeeper must make some tough choices. The first choice for most beekeepers is to use a variety of products from pesticides to essential oils to combat mites. There is plenty of literature on how to treat bees, and even treatment-free beekeepers would be wise to familiarize themselves with these ways and methods. It is always healthy to understand things in life from many different perspectives, even if just to affirm your own. Staying on the treatment-free course, beekeepers have two primary options for dealing with mites.

The first is to do nothing on the bet that the bees will fight the varroa on their own through hygienic behavior, brood breaks[1] and ways we're barely beginning to understand.

The second choice, considered a treatment by some, is to remove the mites' preferred meal: drone brood. Beekeepers will just cut the brood comb out altogether, taking with it a major source of further mite infestation. If you are going to go ahead and cut it out, at least throw it in a pan and fry it up with some olive oil; I hear it's delicious! If that doesn't sound appetizing, you can also put whole frames of drone comb in the freezer to kill everything, but preserve the comb. The bees will clean out the dead brood and you will be able to return to that frame to rinse and repeat. This is impractical for beekeepers with large numbers of hives. It also might be something that seems like a solution on the surface that turns out to create more problems than it solves. While the action in effect removes the varroa, it also removes one aspect of a healthy, fully functioning hive—drones. The stress their absence places on the colony may further weaken the hive, making it even more susceptible to mite-related issues.

By leaving drone comb in the hive, the bees have the opportunity to remove just the infected larvae without destroying the whole drone population. This is of course based

---

1   For more information on brood breaks, refer to page 113.

on the assumption that the bees possess the behaviors necessary to fend off mites, which is certainly not the case with a large number of managed colonies in North America. Most of the bees have not been granted the opportunity to develop the same natural defenses as their feral counterparts. In fact, by treating the bees for mites, in a perverse plot twist, beekeepers actually make the mites *even stronger*. There is no way to completely rid a colony of varroa mites with chemicals or any other measure, so by treating them with chemicals we manage to wipe out the weak mites and leave the strong mites to pass on their treatment resistance to the next generation of mites.

So what is the answer? There isn't one—not in the silver bullet sense anyway. The only answer is to continue to research and be open to new ideas, perspectives and strategies that might emerge from any corner of the beekeeping world. Treatment-free beekeepers shouldn't reject beekeepers who use treatments or ignore any research toward less harmful treatments. This may well be part of the solution for the future of beekeeping. In the same respect, conventional beekeepers must be open and permissive of new beekeepers entering the fray with new ideas. Beekeepers who use treatments on their bees should embrace treatment-free beekeepers as sources of potential solutions and as allies against a common enemy.

HIVE BEETLES

The small hive beetle (SHB) *Aethina tumida* is another invasive pest that has spread to honeybee colonies around the globe. Endemic to sub-Saharan Africa, small hive beetles hitchhiked their way throughout the beekeeping world aboard hives used in migratory beekeeping operations and in colonies exported from their native region. Small hive beetles started showing up in hives in Florida in 1996 and have since spread to over 30 states where they are now found in virtually every beehive. Beekeepers often notice small hive beetles scurrying for cover after removing the hive's top board for inspection and try to squash them before they can disappear among the bees. While they harbor the potential to destroy a honeybee colony, small hive beetles are thought of as a secondary pest. Strong colonies are able to contain the beetle population to manageable levels, but if the hive is weakened as the result of pesticides, mites or poor nutrition the number of beetles can soar and overwhelm a fragile colony.

Small hive beetles are impervious to stingers and like to find little cracks in the hive to hide from the bees who are bent on their eviction. Bees build propolis jails around the beetles to imprison them and prevent them from laying eggs in the combs. When the beekeeper opens the top board, often these

Hive beetle freed from propolis jail

The best defense against small hive beetles is again to maintain strong colonies, remove boxes and consolidate space in the hive to limit unused space, keep entrances reduced, squash any jailed beetles and skip feeding bees protein supplements or pollen patties, as those also feed small hive beetle larvae and will increase the infestation.

beetle prisoners are released back into the hive until the bees can corral them once more. Healthy hives with a sufficient number of bees can prevent beetles from overrunning the colony and spoiling all of their honey in the process.

You can also use a number of commercially available traps that drown beetles in vegetable oil or mineral oil. There are several designs for beetle traps, but they all basically rely on providing an entrance that is big enough for the beetle to hide in but too small for bees to follow suit. The idea is that the bees will chase the beetles into the trap, then the beetles fall into the oil where they drown.

Adult beetles take advantage of unattended comb to lay their eggs, and soon worm-like larvae emerge and start devouring pollen, honey and brood.[1] Larvae spread out over the combs, devouring everything in their paths until leaving the hive to pupate in the soil. While munching their way through larval development, small hive beetles defecate in honey cells, inoculating the cells with yeast spores that ferment and bubble out of the wax cells. Small hive beetle larvae leave the combs covered in a slimy residue and make the honey unfit for human or bee consumption.

Some beekeepers report success in reducing small hive beetle populations by disrupting their pupation in the soil around their hives. Introducing commercially available entomopathogenic nematodes into the soil or spreading diatomaceous earth on the ground around your hives is one way you can manage the levels of small hive beetles. While this approach likely limits the number of beetles pupating near their hives, by design it alters the local soil ecology and does nothing to prevent beetles from flying in from miles around. Beetles are capable of flying impressive distances, and locate colonies by detecting the same scents and pheromones bees use to communicate and navigate.

1   www.extension.org/pages/60425/managing-small-hive-beetles

You can help your bees contain the beetle populations by keeping your bee yard free of scrap combs or dead hives that beetles can exploit, and by maintaining your hiveware so beetles can't easily hide in cracks or slip in through gaps between supers.

Trying to rid the hive of beetles with chemicals disrupts the hive ecology, and paves the way for worse infestation by weakening the colony. Treating an insect colony with insecticide defies logic and contaminates the honey, pollen and wax. Michael Bush puts it best, "I could never bring myself to the idea that it was a good idea to put an insecticide in a colony full of insects and what I consider a food container. As far as I'm concerned, a bee colony is a food container. I expect to get honey out of this colony. Do I want to put insecticides in something I plan to get food out of?"

WAX MOTHS

Galleria mellonella, the greater wax moth, and *Achroia grisella,* the lesser wax moth, are both found throughout North America and Europe. Like small hive beetles, they are thought of as a secondary pest of honeybees. Wax moths proliferate in colonies weakened by disease, pesticides or a failure to requeen. Adult wax moths lay their eggs on abandoned or unguarded combs. The larvae that emerge, called wax worms, burrow through combs and gobble up all the wax, larval casings, pollen and honey in their path.

Wax moths are the recyclers of the hive ecology; by munching their way through combs that have been abandoned by the hive, wax worms free up space for the hive to fill with fresh combs. This is an important function for hives living in natural cavities in trees that are limited by the finite space available for their expansion. Wax moths are much more of a pest for the beekeeper than for the honeybee, as it can be a challenge to prevent them from feeding on frames with drawn comb that isn't being used or guarded by bees.

Beekeepers in areas without true winter like Florida and Southern California have to contend with wax moths throughout each year, whereas beekeepers in colder climates can schedule their honey extractions around the weather. By waiting for the first frost to extract honey, beekeepers can store the empty combs over winter with little fear of providing a wax moth buffet. This is obviously much less of a concern for beekeepers who crush and strain their honey and do not use an extractor.

Wax moths are a symptom of a weak hive, not the cause of the colony's demise. There are no treatments or chemical shortcuts for preventing wax moths from exploiting weak hives and undefended comb. Beekeepers should avoid using moth balls to deter wax moths, as the chemicals are often carcinogenic and contaminate the wax combs. The best defense against wax moths is sound beekeeping practices and maintaining healthy, vigorous hives who can defend their combs.

CHAPTER 6

How to Save a Failing Hive

The prevailing impulse among beekeepers is to provide any assistance they can to help their bees survive, and though well-intentioned, sometimes these efforts only make matters worse. This sense of responsibility to care for their bees is felt most acutely when hives begin displaying signs of poor health and potential failure. Sadly, some hives are destined for failure and cannot be saved despite beekeepers' best efforts to spin a different fate for their bees. Fortunately, many of the most common reasons for weak hives all lead back to the health and vigor of the queen and can be solved or improved by requeening.

Treatment-free beekeepers abhor the modern practice of routinely replacing queens as a standard of care, as would most beekeepers throughout history. However, strategic and judicious use of requeening can resurrect failing hives, change the temperament of overly defensive colonies, give hives brood breaks to reduce mite populations and help beekeepers create additional colonies. Requeening is an important technique for beekeepers to master as the practice can be used to great effect in good times and in bad.

Honeybee queens are obviously central to the health of the hive. They are the member of the colony most responsible for its prosperity—or lack thereof. Queen vigor is the key driver separating weak hives from the hard chargin' hives coveted by all beekeepers.

Much to beekeepers' chagrin, some queens turn out to be duds. A weak queen's inability to raise brood in sufficient quantity makes the hive vulnerable to pressures a strong colony would shrug off with ease. In most cases, replacing weak queens can allow even the most downtrodden of hives to bounce back.

Typically, requeening means locating the existing queen and either killing or removing her from the hive. Her absence will be felt almost immediately and the hive will begin raising replacement queens in peanut-shaped queen cells that extend out from combs in the brood nest. Hives are able to requeen themselves as long as there are fresh eggs in the hive. Queenless hives build emergency queen cells and raise replacement queens from four-day-old larvae. Beekeepers can pull frames of brood and eggs from a strong hive and place them in the queenless hive to ensure they can raise new queens using high-quality larvae from a well-fed colony. Once the queen is removed and the presence of fresh eggs has been confirmed, the bees will take over and instinctively make several new queens.[1] The larvae developing in these specialized queen cells are fed royal jelly

and later hatch as virgin queens, take mating flights and start laying within 24 to 25 days.

Weak or queenless hives can struggle to requeen if they're lacking a sufficient population of workers to forage and defend the hive from intruders while raising the remaining brood until the new queen can start laying an army of her own workers. To help hives through this difficult transition and improve the odds of survival, beekeepers have a surprisingly simple and effective way to instantly supersize the workforce available to help requeen and rebuild the colony.

Once you know the hive needs a queen and has fresh eggs to requeen, you simply swap the hive location of your weak colony with one of your stronger colonies to bolster the weaker population. The strong colony's workers then return home from foraging missions unaware of the house swap that transpired while they were away. All of the strong hive's foragers are oriented to their home coordinates and programmed to return to that exact location after each foraging flight. Returning bees make themselves at home in the replacement hive, and return to business as usual with minimal disruption. Despite sacrificing a significant portion of their foraging force, the strong hive can quickly replenish the ranks and return to full strength in the next few weeks.

1 If multiple virgin queens emerge they will sting each other until only one remains to inherit the "throne." The first queen to hatch often stings her unhatched competitors through their queen cells.

Frame with queen cells

BROOD BREAKS

Whether through swarming, overwintering or requeening, brood breaks serve a critical role in cleansing the hive of brood diseases and parasites. Beekeepers can use this natural tendency to knock down varroa mite populations to a manageable level. Requeening the hive is the easiest way for beekeepers to take advantage of this treatment-free varroa-management strategy. By caging the queen and moving her to another nuc, the hive will immediately start raising replacement queens from young larvae. By the time the virgin queen emerges, mates and starts laying, the hive will have gone broodless long enough to disrupt the varroa reproductive cycle and reduce mite counts significantly.

Induced brood breaks are an important weapon in the fight against varroa, but it is far from the silver-bullet solution to win the battle against such a formidable foe. The chemical warfare beekeepers have been waging against mites has proven to be a spectacular failure resulting in a stronger enemy that is more treatment-resistant each year. Rather than putting evolutionary pressure on the mites to develop treatment resistance and in turn unintentionally breeding super mites, beekeepers must get off the chemical treadmill and start breeding super bees that can stand up to varroa on their own. Instead of selecting for traits like honey production, docility and—of all things—color, bee breeders must prioritize selecting bees that exhibit the hygienic behavior necessary to detect infected brood and dispose of it immediately. There are likely to be several overlapping behaviors and systems bees can use to contain mite populations and the viruses they transmit. The most obvious tactic bees use is to rip out brood they detect is infected with mite larvae and dispose of it far outside the hive. You can occasionally notice your bees engaging in this behavior, with "undertaker bees" carrying white pupae as they fly away from the hive. If you have a chance to inspect the discarded pupae, the immature bee will likely be covered in several small red mites. It can be easy to mistake combs that have had infected brood removed in this manner for "spotty brood" as it makes the queen's laying pattern seem uneven or scattershot.

MEAN BEES–REMOVING A QUEEN

There are also instances when beekeepers need to requeen a hive for their own sake rather than in service of a failing hive. Regardless of genetics or pedigree, all honeybee colonies have the potential to become "too hot" to work. Beekeepers have been selecting against this trait for millennia, opting to breed only bees that are relatively docile when the colony is built up to full strength. Hives can begin life as pliant and gentle and adopt a much more assertive attitude as the colony grows and honey stores increase. The hives' defensive behavior can also escalate throughout the year, particularly during the fall when their pantry is full and everything from bears and badgers to robber bees and beekeepers start showing up looking to swipe their food stores.

Every beekeeper has their own set of criteria for determining what behaviors they are willing to tolerate. These include where the hives are located, how vigorously guard bees respond and how far away from the hive angry bees will follow retreating beekeepers. Generally, there are some pretty clear cut examples of intolerable behavior that necessitate requeening, or in extreme cases, putting the hive down altogether. If the bees flood out of the hive in response to routine inspections handled with good technique, and they make it too dangerous or too unpleasant to work, you should take necessary action to remedy the situation as soon as possible.

The first thing you must know in preparation for requeening a fierce hive is that you are almost certainly going to be stung. Make sure to have abundant fuel for the smoker and be prepared to keep it smoking the whole time. Tape up your pant cuffs, wear appropriate footwear and gloves, and cover any holes in suits and veils before attempting to requeen. Staying hydrated is also important, as bee suits can feel like saunas in the sun. Have Benadryl and an EpiPen on hand in case of an allergy emergency. Putting out signs or warning tape is another good way to prevent innocent bystanders from getting stung.

Moving a hive with a hive carrier (Right)

Finding a queen in a fierce colony can be especially challenging, and can require you to take the hive apart box by box. Obviously bees can find this to be highly objectionable, and will go to great lengths to ensure their feelings on the matter are well understood by you and anyone near the hive. Requeening may not be a viable option for hives located in close proximity to people, pets and livestock, as it can lead to stinging incidents. It is recommended that backyard and urban beekeepers find an "out yard" or remote location where they can move their hives if they become a problem and must be requeened.

Moving a hive of angry bees can be a real challenge on its own, particularly if it weighs a couple hundred pounds. The best time to prepare a hive to move is at night when the entire colony is contained in the hiveware. Once the sun goes down, you can use ⅛ inch hardware cloth to close up the entrance to the hive and enable air circulation while in transit. Cut strips of hardware cloth long enough to cover the hive's entrance and roll or bend them so you can quickly shove them into the gap and staple (or tape) them in place. Any hive boxes and top or bottom boards that are not already screwed or nailed together should be fastened together and wrapped in ratchet straps to prevent your hive from coming apart during the move.

Relocating a large hive is generally a two-person job and is much easier with the use of a hive carrier. Get on either side of the hive—front and back—and get leverage by wedging the hive carrier's metal pegs, which extend from the crossbar into the recessed handholds of the bottom hive box. Lifting up on the handles locks the pegs into the handholds and distributes the weight of the hive between the beekeepers. Once the hive has been moved, it's a good idea to allow your hive to reorient to the new location before attempting to requeen.

Once the safety issues have been addressed, you can start by setting out a bottom board for every box the bees are occupying 20 to 30 feet from the original hive's location. Assuming it hasn't been moved to a new location already, by way of hive carrier, dolly or magic wand, move the whole hive 5 to 10 feet away from the original location. Set an equal number of top boards within reach of the hive. Take ample time to thoroughly smoke the hive by pumping thick plumes through the entrance periodically for several minutes. Place an empty box with top and bottom board in the hive's former location. All of the foragers will return to the empty box where the alarm pheromone is not present and their defensive response is muted as a result.

After another round of heavy smoking, use your hive tool to break the propolis seal between the top two boxes and remove the top box with the top board still in place. Carry the box of bees away from the hive, and set them on one of the bottom boards located 20 to 30 feet away. Smoke the bees off the top of the frames of the next hive box and cover with one of the spare top boards. Repeat the same steps as before until each box has its own top and bottom boards, making sure you use plenty of smoke along the way. Once the hive has been divided up, you can take a much deserved hiatus from the action (ranging from 1 hour to all day). Walk far away from the hive and get rehydrated, eat something, have a rest, take inventory of your health and well-being, go fishing, read a book, write a blog, check Instagram, count your fingers and toes or whatever needs to be done to kill time while the bees settle down for the next phase of requeening.

Giving the bees a break from the smoke allows them to resume normal communication. Workers assemble at the hive entrance and eagerly broadcast the queen's new location by fanning their wings to spread her pheromones through the air. Keep an eye out for fanning behavior[1] as it's a good indication of which box has the queen. The effects of these recruiting efforts should be obvious as the box containing the queen will summon the largest population of bees. The next step in requeening the hive starts with inspecting the box with the most bees.

Place another bottom board next to your most populous box and stack a box without frames on top. Begin the inspection by lightly smoking the bees, remove the top board and study behavior for the telltale signs of the queen.[2] Remove the frame most covered in bees, and carefully inspect the combs for the queen. Place frames that have been ruled out in the empty box and repeat the process with the next most populous frame. Work your way through the box one frame at a time.

Once you spot her majesty, you must act decisively to catch her, as she doesn't stay put for long. You can scoop up queens using special hair-clip-like devices called "queen clip catchers" which help make up for the dexterity lost to gloves. Queen clips, as they are also known, are especially helpful when catching the queen to move her to another hive.

Once you have removed the queen, there are a couple options for how to proceed. The first option is to reassemble the hive entirely and either allow it to requeen naturally and open mate, or try to introduce a queen or queen cell from a breeder[3] and hope the bees accept her as their own. The second option is to divide up the hive's resources to make multiple nucleus colonies, a process beekeepers refer to as "making splits."

---

2   Signs of the queen include the presence of eggs and larvae.

3   To introduce a queen, the caged queen or queen cell should be placed in the middle of two brood nests and disturbed as little as possible for the next two weeks.

---

1   Fanning behavior occurs when worker bees release pheromones that orient bees to the colony. This pheromone is spread by fanning their wings. Bees perch near the hive's entrance with their rear ends in the air and flap their wings vigorously.

EXPANDING YOUR HIVES— MAKING SPLITS

Generally it's not too long after getting the first hive that beekeepers start wanting ten more just like it, and it's at right about this point that family members become convinced the bee fever is real. There are a few factors that lead beekeepers to "need" more hives. The primary reason fueling the need is that once the word gets out to family, friends and neighbors that honey is on the horizon, beekeepers often find their liquid gold is spoken for before their bees have even had a chance to make it. Sometimes beekeepers will have an *actual* need for more hives, beyond the standard desire for more bees and more honey.

Every year beekeepers lose a portion of their colonies over winter to pests, disease, diet, weather, poor management and countless other factors. Some years are worse than others, ranging from minimal losses of 5 to 10 percent in good years, to significant losses of 20 to 40 percent that has been common in recent years and the occasional catastrophic losses of 50 to 100 percent in devastating years. Fortunately, beekeepers can replenish their losses and get more colonies by making splits from their prosperous hives that survived winter.

Sadly, making splits has nothing to do with ice cream, bananas, chocolate sauce or whipped cream. On the bright side, beekeepers can make new colonies by dividing existing hives into splits and then walking away to go get some dessert with the confidence that each split has the resources needed to raise new queens and become full colonies. The "walk away split" is the most effective way for beekeepers to acquire more hives and build them up quickly.

To make a split, transfer one frame of fresh eggs and larvae, two frames of capped brood and two frames of honey and pollen from the original colony, which we'll call Hive A, into a 5-frame nuc box or single deep hive box with top and bottom boards. We'll call this new box Hive B.

You know your hive has either swarmed or is about to swarm if you discover occupied queen cells.[1] In preparation for swarming, hives start raising queens in queen cells and the existing queen flies off with around 60 percent of the hive's workers, usually right after the queen cells are capped. You know the queen cell is capped if it is sealed off to allow the queen to pupate, otherwise it will be uncapped so nurse bees can still feed the developing larvae royal jelly. Never destroy queen cells as a way of preventing swarming—chances are your bees have already swarmed by the time you notice, and you risk leaving the remaining colony queenless with no resources to raise a new queen.

1   Queen cells are specialized cells used to rear queens. The queen cells are peanut-shaped and oriented vertically, rather than horizontally like regular brood cells.

Closely inspect each frame to ensure the queen remains in Hive A, and make sure both hives have sufficient food stores, enough nurse bees to raise brood and eggs and enough young larvae to raise new queens. Now just walk away and allow Hive B to raise queens and Hive A to build back up to full strength. If all goes as planned, you can expect Hive B to have an egg-laying queen within four weeks of the split.

You can expedite this process and get higher-quality queens by taking frames with capped queen cells from hives that are on the verge of swarming. Using already capped queen cells shaves at least eight days off the requeening process and all but guarantees the hive will become queen right. Unlike the "emergency queens" that hives make after suddenly becoming queenless, swarm cell queens are raised by healthy, well-fed hives and have a reputation for being higher quality and longer lasting.

One trick you can use to help ensure Hive B survives the split is to swap locations of Hives A and B, similar to the previously mentioned technique of building up a weak hive. Foragers returning to the newly created colony can help rebuild, restart and requeen. Hive A will eventually reorient to the new location and replenish the workforce it sacrificed for the new

franchise. Hive B benefits from having a full foraging workforce to collect food resources while the colony raises a new queen and rears the next generation of workers. Some beekeepers move Hive A at least two miles away to prevent drift between hives A and B. The distance within an apiary does not make a tremendous difference as long as beekeepers monitor the hives to ensure there is a sufficient population of bees in each. The hives can be placed side by side, and beekeepers can continue to swap locations until the populations even out. It is probably best, though, to place Hive A where it will reside long-term to skip having to reorient the hive to a new location.

Most beekeepers prefer to split hives in the springtime before substantial nectar flows to allow the young colony to gain strength and grow when food resources are abundant. Spring is also when honeybees naturally prefer to split their hives through swarming. It's always best for you to pattern your management practices after the natural behaviors bees evolved over millions of years of trial and error. Rather than seeking to disrupt or prevent your bees' reproductive system, you can split their hive before it swarms to manage the process. This may be especially helpful for urban and backyard beekeepers who want to prevent tens of thousands of bees from flying off all at once.

MATED QUEENS

Rather than waiting for splits to raise their own queens, commercial beekeepers commonly introduce mated queens to get brood production started faster and with fewer uncertainties. The term "mated queen" in this context refers to lab-inseminated queens produced by queen-rearing operations. Commercial beekeepers seek to maximize honey production and increase the number of hives available for pollination services, and their mated queens start laying eggs three weeks ahead of naturally raised, open-mated queens. Much to the beekeepers dismay, however, hives will often reject mated queens or replace her at their first chance without regard for her pedigree or price tag.

HOW TO PREVENT SWARMING

As the spring season gets kicked off, hives take stock of the previous year's success and decide collectively whether the colony is capable of reproducing successfully. Once consensus has been reached, hives build swarm cells and begin rearing queens. The existing queen leads a mass exodus from the hive in search of a new cavity space to colonize. Swarming is when the hive's queen leaves with the majority of worker bees in search of a new hive, leaving behind a contingent of worker bees and a virgin queen to restart the colony. Imagine up to 50,000 bees flying at once in a spectacular display of reproduction, swirling and buzzing about completely oblivious to the number of humans they've undoubtedly sent scurrying indoors.

Queens need empty frames to lay eggs.

These empty honeycomb cells will be used for food storage or brood rearing.

Honeybee colonies swarm to both reproduce the colony and relieve overcrowding in the brood nest. When hives run out of space to expand food storage, cells in the brood nest the queen would otherwise fill with eggs are repurposed and refilled with nectar. Eventually, the queen runs out of space to lay her eggs and the brood nest gets congested with activity. In addition to making bees grumpy, overcrowding inspires the hive to make queen cells and initiate swarming.

RELIEVING CONGESTION IN THE BROOD NEST

You can prevent overcrowding by placing undrawn frames between combs in the brood nest and adding new hive boxes—supers—to provide plenty of additional space for nectar storage. Move the drawn frames you removed from the brood nest and replaced with the undrawn frames into the center of the new box you are adding on top of the existing hive boxes. By moving brood frames up into the new box, bees are drawn upward to care for the brood. This alerts the colony that there is plenty of room for expansion. Adding a top entrance to the hive can also help cut down the traffic in the brood nest. Use a bottom board in place of your top board to add another entrance for the bees, but be sure to use an entrance reducer[1] to limit the amount of space your bees have to guard from hive beetles, wax moths, ants, humans and so on.

1   Entrance reducers are barriers placed at the entrance of the hive to reduce the opening to the size of about two or three bees.

SPLITTING SWARMS

There is very little beekeepers can do to convince their bees to change course once they've begun preparing to swarm. Destroying swarm cells only prolongs the inevitable swarm and risks leaving the remaining hive without a replacement queen. Beekeepers can simply collect the swarm (see "How to Catch a Swarm," p. 68), if they are fortunate enough to catch their bees in the act. Since that is not always possible, splitting the hive is the next best option.

Upon discovering capped queen cells, you can simply split your hive—Hive A—and place any frames with queen cells along with one or two frames of capped brood and plenty of nurse bees, and at least two frames of honey and pollen into the new hive—Hive B—for food. You can actually split the hive as many times as resources permit. If she hasn't swarmed already, the existing queen will continue to lay eggs in Hive A, and the queen cells in Hive B will hatch within eight days of being capped. The new queen will start laying eggs twelve days after emerging from her queen cell.

Beekeepers swap locations of hives to more closely simulate swarming by removing the original queen and leaving behind capped queen cells just as if she had left on her own accord. Keep an eye on the original hive to be sure the queen sticks around and resumes laying eggs. If she did leave, you can simply add a frame of fresh eggs from another hive and the bees will raise a new queen. The new hive may issue secondary swarms with smaller groups leaving with one or several of the virgin queens as they are expelled from the hive.

Comb with open brood and fresh eggs (Left)

CHAPTER 7

Nectar Flow, Beebread What to Feed Your Bees

Nutrition is the number one key to honeybee health, and there is no substitute for honey and pollen. Honeybees thrive when nectar and pollen are flowing from a diversity of sources and struggle when their diet is compromised by poor weather or artificial feed. While plants produce nectar and pollen at various times throughout the year, most production takes place in the spring months and the rest blooms intermittently throughout the summer and fall. Beekeepers refer to spring as the "honey flow" or "nectar flow" and look forward to it all winter because it is when their bees are healthiest and most productive.

Beekeepers with access to a variety of bee yards often transport their bees between them to position their hives to take advantage of the various nectar flows throughout the seasons. Bee yards in close proximity to monocultures or areas of low plant biodiversity can be problematic; after the spring flourish, those planted acres become virtual food deserts for honeybees. Outside of the brief window when the crop is in bloom, the area produces no food resources for bees.

Spring is literally the sexiest time of the year. As winter recedes and the days grow longer, nature emerges from slumber to begin the season of creation. The gradual increase in soil and air temperatures stimulates the germination of seeds and the growth of flowers, which of course means the production of pollen and nectar. Flowers blossom from amorous plants and disperse their grains of pollen, male haploid gametophytes, through the wind and aboard pollinators. Flowers glow in ultraviolet light like neon signs to the insect eye, advertising their supremely sweet and seductively scented nectar with patterns and designs that pollinators find irresistible. After luring them to blossoms with sensuous floral marketing, plants whet the bees' appetite with just enough ambrosia to inspire subsequent visits to other blossoms of the same species. In exchange for their nutritious nectar, plants enlist bees in their sex lives to help share their genetic material—pollen—among members of their species. This transaction of swapping pollen and nectar for pollination results in plant reproduction and the creation of food for humans and countless other species. In essence, honeybees are flying extensions of plants' reproductive organs, allowing organisms that are rooted to one specific location to have sex with partners distributed over vast expanses of land.

Beekeepers refer to the times of the year when pollen and nectar sources have dried up as the "dearth." During this time, hives can start running into problems. Rather than having to feed their bees, beekeepers will move their hives in search of greener pastures, chasing the honey flow. To seek out the best locations for your hives, you should become an amateur botanist and familiarize yourself with local floral resources and their nutritional value for your bees. Health of honeybee colonies is inexorably tied to their nutrition, and as beekeepers it is our job to seek out the best habitat and forage for our bees.

The problem is, moving bees places stress upon the colony, which can make the hive all the more vulnerable to parasites, pesticides and pathogens. Beyond the disruption of having the hive closed up and bounced around en route, once your bees arrive at their new location they have to totally relearn their surroundings, recalibrate their internal GPS systems to their new location and immediately find sources of food and water. From my experience, moves can often cause the bees to "blame the queen" for the disruption, which results in swarming or queen supersedure. If the colony senses the queen is failing, whether because of age, injury, disease, or in this case, the disruption, they will replace her by raising virgin queens and killing her upon their maturity. This process has both positive

Honeybees feed on the nectar in flower blossoms. (Right)

and negative effects. On one hand the replacement of the queen gives the hive a brood break, which disrupts the varroa mites' reproductive cycle and limits their population. On the other hand it limits the hive's productivity as the population decreases significantly for an almost month-long absence of a laying queen. Finding bee yards that provide steady nutrition throughout the year without supplemental feeding or relocation is a top goal for beekeepers. This has increasingly meant locations in or near urban environments.

A poor diet makes bees all the more vulnerable to parasites, pesticides, disease and stress. Feeding honeybees syrup likely disrupts the lactic acid bacteria (LAB),[1] which live in the honey stomach of bees, an organ that serves a critical role in food production. The microbiota inhabiting the honey stomach is dominated by several phylotypes of *Lactobacillus* and *Bifidobacterium*. These colonies of lactic acid bacteria help ferment nectar into honey and pollen into beebread,[2] and these same microbes play a key role in the health of the colony by suppressing the growth of pathogens and parasites. This ancient symbiotic relationship evolved over at least seventy million years with both species thriving by exploiting mutually beneficial food sources. For all but a blip on this evolutionary timeline, the stability of their food sources—nectar and pollen—allowed for the successful marriage of bee and bacterium.

The bounty of this flourishing marriage is honey. Bees collect nectar and store it in their honey stomach where lactic acid bacteria begin to brew it into honey. The bees then return to the hive and regurgitate the nectar into a wax cell where it will continue to ferment and dehydrate until it becomes honey. Nectar is a complex chemical cocktail composed of sucrose, glucose and fructose, in addition to a large variety of complementary amino acids, lipids, antioxidants, alkaloids and phenolic substances.[3] Bees receive tremendous nutritional and immunological benefits from these complex sugars, amino acids and assorted chemicals, all of which are lost when beekeepers substitute the honeybees' natural food with syrup.

In contrast to nectar, syrup is typically pure sucrose and the product of mixing granulated white cane sugar and water at a ratio of 1:1 or 2:1. Syrup is typically neutral at pH 7+, whereas nectar ranges in pH from 4.2 to 8.5.[4] Honey consistently has an average pH of 3.9 and is considerably acidic. It is possible that the increased alkalinity of syrup is disruptive to the delicate balance of the hives' ecosystems, from the microbiota living in bees' honey stomach to the microbes responsible for brood diseases. According to Michael Bush, "Many of the honeybee's enemies, such as Nosema, chalkbrood, European foulbrood and varroa all thrive and reproduce better at the pH of sugar syrup and don't reproduce well at the pH of honey."

1   http://journals.plos.org/plosone/article?id=10.1371/journal.pone.0033188
2   http://ijs.sgmjournals.org/content/64/Pt_9/3109.full.pdf

3   https://hal.archives-ouvertes.fr/file/index/docid/890439/filename/hal-00890439.pdf
4   https://hal.archives-ouvertes.fr/file/index/docid/890439/filename/hal-00890439.pdf

This mixture of sugar and water also lacks the complimentary chemicals found in nectar. While syrup is technically a solution, it is not *the* solution for keeping healthy bees. In fact, feeding syrup creates as many problems as it solves.

Feeding has the potential to do the following:

1. *set off robbing*

2. *attract ants and other pests*

3. *create brood nest congestion and set off swarming*

4. *result in the drowning of countless bees*

In spite of all the negative aspects, feeding can help a weak hive or package survive a dearth of pollen and nectar. In the event your hives are in jeopardy of starvation, it is an important skill for you to possess.

Making simple syrup is easy enough—add sugar to boiling water until dissolved, and then let cool—but getting the ratios correct can be a little tricky. Michael Bush advises measuring your sugar and water separately for accurate mixtures. His simple formula is one pound of sugar for every pint of water. In order to make 1:1 syrup, you mix equal measures in pounds of sugar and pints of water. In order to make 2:1 syrup, you add two pounds of sugar for every pint of water. For example, to make 2:1 syrup from a twenty pound bag of sugar, you add it to ten pints of boiling water and stir until thoroughly dissolved.

Since syrup is on average more alkaline than nectar, you can add Vitamin C, ascorbic acid and citric acid to lower the pH of the mixture. This also helps prevent the syrup from spoiling and can make it more appealing to the bees. There isn't a simple formula to achieve the desired pH level. Instead, you have to test using digital pH meters or good old-fashioned test strips and adjust accordingly. The best advice is to add small amounts and test frequently to prevent bringing the pH down too far.

Beekeepers use different ratios for different times of year, but again, everyone has their own recipe for feeding bees. The common practice to encourage brood rearing in the spring before the flow starts is by feeding bees 1:1 syrup. To help bees stock up on honey for the winter, feed them 2:1 in the fall. Depending on their location and the time of year new packages arrive, beekeepers may have to feed their bees until local pollen and nectar sources return. If it is warm enough for the bees to break cluster and take the syrup, plants that they prefer and are better for the colony are likely to be blooming nearby. The early buildup of brood that results from early spring feeding can be problematic in the event of a late frost or prolonged poor weather conditions. The brood can be damaged by the cold snap, or the early buildup may result in swarming from an overcrowded brood nest.

Fall feeding begins with the practice of harvesting the colony's natural honey stores and replacing them with artificial feed and "funny honey" for the bees to eat over winter.[1] This is a

---

1 "Funny honey" refers to products that are labeled as honey but are mostly made from corn syrup or other additives.

strategy destined for hardship. You should *always* leave your bees enough real honey to survive well into spring. Failure to do so means the bees will almost certainly need to be fed in the spring. This starts their year off at a disadvantage, as they might not build up enough and will have to be fed all through the fall to survive another winter.

The amount of honey that your bees will need to make it through winter depends on the variety of bees and the duration and severity of the seasons in your region. A good target weight for the hive is between 100 to 150 pounds.[1] However, a hive that weighs slightly less but is full of real honey is perfect and doesn't need to be pumped up with artificial feed to hit an arbitrary target weight. As you evaluate your hives in the fall and thoughts of harvesting honey run through your brain, it would be wise for you to remember one of the most important principles of beekeeping backwards: beekeeping is not about honey!

BAGGIE FEEDER APPROACH

There comes a time in every beekeeper's journey when they must consider whether to feed their bees or leave them to face starvation on their own. If sharing resources from other hives is impossible, most beekeepers will elect to feed their bees syrup as a last resort. There are practically 101 ways to feed bees syrup, most of which are better suited for large-scale beekeeping operations. The best method for small-scale beekeepers is,

incidentally, the most safe and effective of them all. All that is required for the "baggy feeder" approach is:

- ✔ *cooled syrup*
- ✔ *1-gallon freezer bag*
- ✔ *2-inch wood shim*
- ✔ *razor blade or sharp knife*

Fill half of the gallon bag with cooled syrup and make sure it's sealed; a baggie that opens en route to the bee yard will cause a sticky mess! Next, remove the top board and place the shim[2] on top of the hive. Lay the bag of syrup on top of the frames and cut a few slits in the top of the bag with a sharp blade. Place the top board on the shim to close up the hive. The shim provides enough separation between the top bars of the frames and the top board to allow the bees to walk on top of the baggie and drink from the slits.

The baggie feeder method drastically reduces the number of bees who drown attempting to drink syrup, especially compared to frame feeders. Also, placing the syrup at the very top of the hive reduces the risk of robbing, as robber bees would have to fight through the entire hive to get to the syrup. Bees are perfectly willing to wage that kind of campaign, but the chances are far less than when using feeders that drip the syrup right at the hive's entrance. Beekeepers should *always* reduce their entrances when feeding to make it more challenging for robber bees to invade and plunder the product of the hive's hard work.

1   You can purchase a hive scale to weigh your hives, but for the common backyard beekeeper this is a bit of overkill.

2   A shim is a ¾-inch rectangular frame placed on top of hive boxes and below the top board to enable baggy feeding.

Bees store nectar and pollen in cells to feed on during the winter. (Right)

POLLEN PARTICLES

Another way beekeepers supplement their bees' diet is with pollen and, more commonly, pollen substitutes or "pollen patties." Bees prefer fresh, live pollen to pollen collected from traps or patties and are unlikely to take the latter if the former is available. Pollen patties are made from recipes you can easily find online. They include ingredients like brewers' yeast, sugar, dried egg powder, lemon juice and water. Note that they usually contain no actual pollen.

Foraging worker bees return to the hive to unload their colorful cargo and are met by young bees who receive the pellets in their pollen baskets. The pollen is combined with honey, royal jelly, enzymes and saliva and inoculated with microbes living on the bees' heads, which they use to ram pollen into wax cells for storage. Bees follow this ancient recipe in order to ferment raw pollen into beebread. Also known as brood food, beebread is the main nutritional resource fueling brood rearing and contributing to the health and prosperity of the hive. Nurse bee's diet of beebread allows them to produce the royal jelly that they feed to young larvae. Beebread is also fed to brood directly to power their metamorphosis from larvae to pupae to full-fledged honeybee.

Beebread made from patties is nutritionally inferior to natural pollen, even if it has been enhanced with all manner of boosters, vitamins and enzymes. Given the choice between feeding patties or starvation, most beekeepers will choose the former and hope for the best. You can feed patties in similar fashion to baggie feeding, with a shim providing the room to lay the patties on a sheet of wax paper on the top bars of the uppermost hive box.

Alternatively, beekeepers can feed their bees real pollen, which they typically obtain from pollen traps placed on hives during previous pollen flows. The nutritional value of pollen diminishes rapidly, so it must be immediately fermented or frozen—preferably freeze-dried. Culturing lactic acid bacteria along with pollen, honey and water in an airtight container will produce beebread-like fermented pollen. You can also just freeze-dry pollen and let the bees "bake" the beebread themselves.

Pollen is more sensitive to humidity and temperature than syrup or patties and may not be appealing to bees unless it meets their Goldilocks-like set of criteria. To prevent it from spoiling or becoming unappetizing, beekeepers can put pollen or beebread in a dish on top of a queen excluder or an old screened bottom board and leave it there until the bees eat it all or lose interest.

To "open-feed" dry pollen, beekeepers can place pollen inside an otherwise empty hive in exactly the same manner as if feeding directly. This shelters the pollen from the elements and limits its introduction into the hive's ecology if the bees are not interested. Open feeders are usually fairly low-tech and one is generally enough for at least 50 hives. There are as many open feeder designs available online as there are opinions on "how things ought to be done."

Beekeepers can purchase dry pollen in bulk to feed their bees, however, all of the commercially available pollen has been irradiated to kill any infectious spores like American foulbrood. Obviously bees would much prefer to collect living pollen, but will take irradiated pollen in a pinch. They'll also collect sawdust if they are hungry enough. After being hit with gamma rays, pollen is sterilized and lacks both beneficial and nefarious microbes. Fresh pollen is teeming with microbiological life and is far more nutritious and immunologically beneficial than irradiated pollen. Much of the commercially available irradiated pollen is imported from China, which raises concerns of pesticide contamination.

Backwards beekeepers don't use queen excluders—devices that prevent queens from accessing boxes above the brood nest in order to separate honeycomb from combs used to raise brood. Excluders are like grills that fit over the boxes of the brood nest with bars that are wide enough for workers to slip through but too small for the queen to pass. If the queen can't get past the excluder, she can't lay eggs in the boxes above; instead they will be used exclusively for honey storage. This makes the beekeeper's job easy when it comes time to harvest, but is also a good way for your bees to get overcrowded and swarm. Worker bees want to go where it smells like the queen and the excluder deliberately prevents the queen and her smell from passing into the boxes above. Hives will make a queen excluder situation work, but they create unnecessary stress—stress that is imposed for the beekeeper's sake entirely.

FEEDING PRECAUTIONS

Feeding bees pollen and patties early in the spring and late in the fall is a strategy that ignores the very first principle of beekeeping backwards: Work with Nature, not against Her. In most climates, honeybees drastically reduce the size of their brood nest as fall approaches and don't build back up again until nectar and pollen start flowing in the springtime.

Beekeepers feed their bees pollen to encourage brood rearing and boost the population of bees. Stimulative feeding aims to send hives into the spring honey flow and winter hibernation with the largest population of bees possible, during times when hives would otherwise have much lower populations. Feeding tricks the hive into expanding the brood nest by simulating a pollen flow, but as the population grows, so do the demands placed upon the hive. In contrast to honeybees' natural brood-rearing cycle, this population growth places stress on the hive right when it is least able to cope. Large populations going into winter means more mouths to feed and brood to care for, which increases the likelihood the hive will run out of food or freeze before the spring flow returns. Broodless clusters are able to maintain at much lower temperatures—70°F or 21°C—which allows them to use energy and food resources much more efficiently. Hives that are raising brood must maintain a much higher temperature of 94°F or 34°C. With little or no help from the sun, hives must expend tremendous amounts of energy and food to keep the brood warm enough to survive the chilly temperatures.[1] Similarly, a booming population of bees with brood production in full swing before pollen and nectar start flowing will burn through remaining resources and likely swarm.

Stimulative feeding creates hives that are out of sync with the natural cycles and systems that have enabled honeybees to thrive for millions of years. The natural ebb and flow in the population of bees within the colony is not an inconvenience, it's a system that has allowed bees to survive winter and control pests long before humans arrived on the scene. The natural growth and contraction of the bee population that corresponds to seasonal resources provides a rejuvenating and much deserved brood break for the queen. Brood breaks not only give the queen some time off from laying eggs, it also breaks the varroa mites' brood-rearing cycle. With no vulnerable brood to feast on all winter, varroa are unable to reproduce and populations are drastically reduced. Without this brood break, varroa populations are allowed to continue their exponential expansion. Keep in mind that if you are feeding your bees to boost the population of your hive, you are also raising the varroa who prey on the brood your bees are raising by providing them with food and shelter inside capped brood cells.

1   *Honey Bee Biology and Beekeeping, Revised Edition,* by Dewey M. Caron

Urban gardens are a great way to naturally support bees' nutrition.

PLANTING POLLINATOR FORAGE

Rather than moving hives or providing syrup and pollen patties, the best way beekeepers can support their bees' nutritional needs is to plant pollinator forage within range of their bee yard. In fact, creating pollinator habitat is the best way to support pollinators and the security of our food supply. Beekeeping is not for everyone, but food certainly is and that means we all have a stake in protecting our pollinators. For every beekeeper who takes up the mantle and responsibility of personally looking after honeybees, there are 1,000—maybe even 10,000—gardeners who are eager get their hands dirty and provide forage and habitat for pollinators of every stripe.

It is likely that everyone has encountered a bush or tree buzzing loudly with bees and noticed worker bees zipping from blossom to blossom. Gardeners often observe such feeding frenzies with jealousy, wishing the bees would show the same kind of enthusiasm for their tomato blossoms. Watching bees fixate on one flowering plant over another, especially when the two are side by side, can be extremely frustrating to a green thumb hoping for a bumper crop. As true connoisseurs of nectar, bees are highly opinionated and have very strong dining preferences.

For starters, from a honeybee's perspective, not all flowers are created equal. Flowering plants vary from one species to another in the amount of nectar and pollen produced by each blossom, and bees are able to gain access to these food resources to varying degrees due to the size, shape and design of each flower. Many nectar-producing plants that require direct pollination coevolved their floral structures to suit a specific pollinator and often their flowers are shaped to accommodate the pollinator's unique anatomy.

Plants with mutations that make them more appealing to pollinators are more likely to reproduce and pass on their genetic advantage to their offspring. Since this coevolutionary relationship began, flowers have been outdoing themselves to attract the attention of picky pollinators to increase reproductive success. Lucky for us, this has resulted in spectacularly beautiful and fragrant flowers for us to enjoy.

Among the benefits of planting honeybee forage and pollinator habitat are the magnificent colors and aromas they can bring to any landscape. This is important because people value beauty and will care for and protect the things they value. Fortunately, many of the plants bees find most irresistible also happen to be aesthetically pleasing to the human eye. We share a mutual appreciation for plants as they burst with colorful flowers, swell with sweet ambrosia and beckon us to their blossoms with intoxicating aromas and inspiring designs. Unlike humans, however, honeybees have a real soft spot for weeds and will pollinate invasive species as eagerly as the native species the weeds seek to replace. When considering plant species to cultivate for honeybee forage and pollinator habitat, beekeepers must be careful not to introduce invasive plants that spread and displace native plant communities and cause untold agricultural damage.

Luckily, there are countless resources online[1] to research the impressive number of plants bees prefer to visit and the relative value of each plant species for honey production. Every opportunity to plant forage and create habitat is unique and the best combination of plants varies greatly depending on location, resources and intention. A primary consideration when selecting forage plants is whether they are hardy enough to survive the local climate, air temperatures, soil conditions, elevation and so on. The best and most practical way to select forage plants that thrive under local conditions while carrying zero risk of disrupting ecosystems is to choose only plants native to the area. Native plants evolved to thrive in the local climate and make efficient use of the soil and water resources available. Native plants have the added bonus of supporting native bees, bumblebees, butterflies, beetles, birds and every native creature standing to benefit from the restoration of their natural habitat.

1   www.honeylove.org/resources

In addition to natives, beekeepers can also use a huge variety of noninvasive plant species from other areas of the world with similar climates to add some serious nectar-producing ringers to the local lineup. Drought-tolerant non-native plants can sometimes be a preferred choice to a native alternative on water-conservation grounds alone, especially if they produce nectar in greater abundance.

The time of year a plant's nectar starts flowing is equally, if not more, important than the amount of nectar a plant produces. While it is always helpful to have an extra-strong spring flow, selecting a combination of plants that bloom all at once during the time of greatest abundance is no good to the bees later in the year when the flow dries up and forage becomes scarce. Consider choosing a combination of plants that bloom in successive waves to supplement the bees' diet more evenly throughout the beekeeping year.

Urban and suburban beekeepers already benefit from the diversity of plant life proliferating in the gardens and green spaces throughout city environments. The same trees, bushes, hedgerows, edibles and flower gardens that provide our urban communities with shade, fresh air, food and natural beauty also produce some of the best nutritional resources for honeybees in the highest concentrations. Beekeepers in city environments also have the added benefit of large recruiting pools—friends and neighbors—to enlist in planting forage and creating habitat for pollinators.

To find the best pollinator plants and honeybee forage, consult your local university's agriculture department, and visit:

– *www.xerces.org/pollinator-conservation/plant-lists/*
– *pollinator.org/guides.htm*
– *www.wildflower.org/explore.php·*
– *www.cnps.org*

In the Los Angeles area, we love:

– *theodorepayne.org/*
– *www.matilijanursery.com*

CHAPTER 8

How to Prepare Hives for Winter

New beekeepers often get frustrated when their questions continue to be answered with the refrain, "Well, it depends…." That's because there are few management strategies that are universally appropriate for every beekeeping scenario. Locality is one of the greatest variables to account for when determining the best course of action to help your hives prosper. The degree to which you have to prepare your hives for winter will of course depend on where your hives are located.

As Southern Californian beekeepers, wintering our bees is not a huge concern. When most of the country's beehives are under several feet of snow, our bees are foraging on eucalyptus and the other southern hemisphere plants that bloom here during winter months. I'm much more concerned with getting them through the hottest months of summer and fall until the rains return. I just make sure my bees have plenty of honey and pollen to survive the dearth, and remove any unoccupied boxes.

I've noticed my queens often take a natural brood break during this time, which helps cut down the mite population and ensures they will have enough honey to make it until the nectar flow returns.

The best way to figure out how to overwinter bees in your location is to learn what strategies have been effective for local mentors who have been successful in the past. This underscores the need for you to find a community to help learn the many tips and tricks that work in the local environment, including which bees are best adapted for the area.

There is no universal answer for the amount of honey you need to leave on your hives to overwinter your bees. As a general principle, however, the more honey you leave on the hive, the better. In addition to helping protect bees from starvation, honey insulates the hive from the freezing temperatures.

In regions with cold, wet and snowy winters, maintaining air flow throughout the hive is important—condensation can be a killer. Adding a small top entrance (see "How to Prevent Swarming," p. 120) to the hive can be enough to keep air circulating and prevent dangerous humidity from accumulating. Some beekeepers go so far as to nudge their boxes slightly off kilter to create drafts throughout the stack.

Tilting the hive slightly forward ensures that any moisture that collects can flow out the entrance. You can also put two pennies on either side of your top hive box to lift the top board just enough to allow some airflow. Insulated top covers can be helpful in areas where the hive is likely to be covered in snow for extended periods. Beekeepers can also set up wind breaks to spare their hives from the worst of it. Reducing bottom entrances helps prevent gusts of cold air from whipping through the hive. Beekeepers can even bring their bees into shelters like barns or root cellars as long as bees can still take cleansing flights[1] on mild days.

In instances where their bees might otherwise starve, beekeepers will feed syrup in early spring and during the fall. Bees that have had access to proper nutritional resources and have been well managed by the beekeeper should have no problem making enough honey to overwinter. Syrup makes a lousy substitute for real honey and can influence the health of the entire colony. Feeding can introduce a whole host of other problems that may ultimately prove fatal to the colony, so it may be a better strategy to combine weaker colonies or borrow frames of drawn honey from stronger hives to supplement their diet instead. Rather than trying to find ways to subvert honeybees' natural diet, beekeepers must prioritize their hive's nutritional needs above all else.

1 When outside temperatures are above 50°F or 10°C, bees take cleansing flights to excrete waste. Bees do not defecate inside the hive.

In winter, bees in warm climates can continue foraging from flowers. (Right)

In cold climates, though, you can help your bees survive by maintaining proper airflow in the hive and by ensuring the bees have enough honey to eat.

CHAPTER 9

Honey Harvest

As long as humans have walked the earth, our species has been fascinated by honey and has gone to unbelievable lengths to revel in its sweetness. You can imagine the epic tales told around a campfire of the hero who risked life and limb to snatch the sweet nectar of the gods for all to enjoy from a hive loaded with bees. One can speculate how valuable honey would have been to early humans, considering nothing at the time could compare to the mouthwatering sweetness of honey. It's not like you could just stop off at the 7-Eleven to grab a Slurpee®. Readers who know how crazy kids get for sweets can picture the bonanza plundered honey would have created in a time before Oreo® and Cap'n Crunch©. Children would have idolized anyone brave enough to take on the role of honey hunter. It's also fun to think that our species—Homo sapiens—probably was not the first hominid to catch bee fever. Surely Neanderthals were clever enough and curious enough to have discovered honey and valued it enough to endure whatever stings resulted from a raid. Ever since those early raids, humans have been fixated on getting more and more honey.

Clearly honey has always held tremendous economic value and that has been a motivating factor, but for most of history honey was too rare and treasured to exploit on any scale. Honey is the motivating factor that has forever compelled humans to experiment with honeybees, hoping to tame a wild creature and train its instincts to suit our purposes, often at our own peril.

Every beekeeper should keep pushing the envelope and experimenting with bees. Rather than fixing an end goal only on increased honey production, beekeepers should experiment with ways to minimize the impact we have on hives though our interactions. Harvesting honey is a process that has the potential to be quite disruptive to the hive; however, there are a few tricks to save your bees unnecessary unpleasantness.

The main consideration when trying to remove honey from a hive—that would much rather you didn't—is how to get the bees off the combs you want to harvest. Beekeepers have answered this several ways; some simply brush the bees off the comb and back into their hive, others use a chemical so repulsive to bees that they fly as far and as fast as possible away from it. Brushes get the job done when harvesting a frame or

two, but are impractical for larger quantities. Plus, as you can imagine, bees sometimes take issue with being flicked off their comb and go looking for someone to blame.

ESCAPE BOARDS

A more effective, albeit slower, method of harvesting uses an escape board. An escape board is a two-inch shim exactly the same dimensions as your hive box with a flat board attached to the top. At the center of the board is a one- to two-inch hole. The underside of the board, which is touching the shim, has the "escape" portion of the contraption. Think of the escape as a one-way door that channels bees through several exits just large enough for a bee to squeeze out, but too small to crawl back through.

Escape board designs vary but serve the same purpose. When making your selection, be sure there are multiple outlets so traffic does not back up if one bee gets stuck. Place the bee escape between the rest of the hive and the box—or boxes—you intend to harvest. Be careful to make sure the queen is in the boxes below the escape board; she is too large to fit through the escape. Any bees remaining in the boxes above the escape board will find their way out and rejoin the rest of the hive or set out on a foraging mission. With the one-way door in place, the bees

When the time comes to harvest honey, we use an escape board to clear the box of bees.

An escape board seperates honey super from the rest of the hive. (Right)

cannot get back into the boxes separated by the escape board once they leave. When you return to the hive after a while, from a few hours to a day or two, you can take off the boxes above the escape board and they will be virtually free of bees.

There are a couple things to be aware of when using an escape board. The first is that you must be sure that the one-way door leads in the right direction. If it is put on upside down, bees will get trapped in the boxes with nowhere to go. As you can imagine, opening a blockaded box would not be an enjoyable experience. Also, before you walk away from installing your escape board, it pays to triple check that there is no brood in the box you intend to harvest and that the queen hasn't snuck in there as well. Bees have a tendency to store their honey in the top boxes; you can move frames of honey up when adding boxes to harvest later. Finally, it's also important that you not let too much time pass between putting on the escape board and returning to harvest the honey, because you can be sure that ants will have sniffed out the honey and helped themselves to it. Unfortunately, ants are much harder to get off honeycombs than bees.

Beekeepers have also reported success using an empty box in lieu of an escape board. The goal is the same: to remove a box full of honey without any bees. In this case, rather than trapping them out of the box with the escape mechanism, you are relying on the bees' preference for being near the brood nest

to trick them to abandon the honey boxes. Bees are drawn to the brood nest by the queen's pheromone and the smell of the brood. Because there is an empty box between the honey box and the rest of the hive, the bees may leave the combs in the honey box to go on foraging missions or to be closer to the rest of the hive. The empty box breaks the continuity of the combs that the bees will then consider to be the top of their hive—even though there is a whole box of honey just inches above.

BOTTLING

Pulling boxes of honey off hives is the easy part and just the beginning of the very sticky process of bottling the product of your bees' hard work. Before even considering harvesting honey, it is necessary for the beekeeper to have the appropriate equipment to process honey from comb to jar. Otherwise they are bound to create a spectacular mess, wasting honey in the process. Large beekeeping outfits often fully mechanize their process for getting honey out of the combs and into sealed containers, with hot knives slicing off wax cappings and centrifuge extractors spinning the honey out of each wax cell and into a collection chamber where it is heated, and then fed through a pipe into vats. They are then poured into jars through a spigot. This level of sophistication is neither within reach or desirable for small-scale beekeepers. Fortunately, there is an ultra-cheap, do-it-yourself alternative that makes the process even more exciting—and delicious!

Paint strainer in straining bucket

Wrapping duct tape around paint strainer in straining bucket

The "crush and strain" method is the most low-tech and easy way to get your honey into cute little bottles, and just as the name implies, it involves crushing up the honeycombs and straining honey from the wax. To construct your DIY crush-and-strain system you'll need:

- *three white 5-gallon food-grade plastic buckets with lids*
- *one ½-inch plastic spigot*
- *at least one open 5-gallon elastic paint strainer bag, available at any hardware store*
- *power drill*
- *½-inch unused drill bit*

- *⅛-inch unused drill bit*
- *box cutter or blade*
- *duct tape*
- *paint scraper on wooden pole*

The three buckets each have their own purpose; one is used for crushing up the honeycombs to release the honey, the second is used to strain the resulting slurry of honey and wax into the third bucket, where it collects before being poured into jars through the plastic spigot. The crushing bucket requires no preparation.

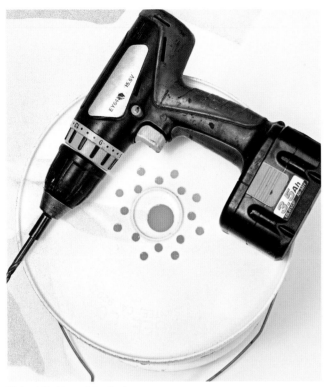

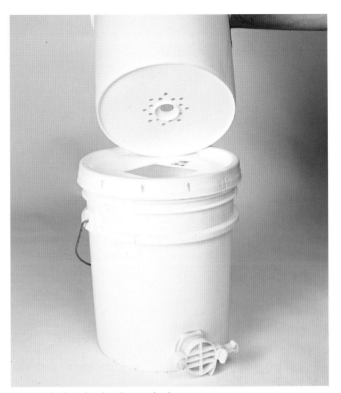

Holes drilled in straining bucket

Straining bucket placed on bottom bucket

To prepare the second bucket for straining, drill at least a dozen holes into the bottom of the bucket near the center with the ⅛-inch drill bit. Clean out any plastic bits and sanitize with an iodine solution. Next, put the paint strainer bag inside the bucket and drape the elastic around the outside of the bucket far enough so the bottom of the bag is several inches from the bottom of the bucket. Wrap duct tape tightly around the outside of the edge of the bucket to hold the strainer firmly in place. Next, using the clean ½-inch drill bit, drill a hole as far down the side of the third bucket as possible. The plastic spigot should fit snuggly in the hole and is locked in place with a plastic nut from inside the bucket. Finally, using a box cutter or blade, cut a circle from the center of a plastic lid big enough not to block drips from any of the holes drilled in the bottom of the second bucket. The second bucket will be sitting on top of the lid, so it is important that you remove only as much of the lid as is necessary. Be sure to wash everything with an iodine solution before use.

Crush and strain bucket set up

Getting ready to cut honeycomb into crushing buckets

Cutting honeycomb out of frame

Crushing honeycomb with paint scraper

Crushed honey poured into straining bucket

Bottling honey

The crushing part of the process is by far the most satisfying, especially for anyone who enjoys the weird pleasure of popping bubble wrap, smashing ice in frozen puddles or peeling the cling wrap off new electronics. Once all of the buckets are prepared and assembled, the next order of business is to cut the combs from the frames into the crushing bucket. Using the paint scraper on a wooden handle, thoroughly crush all the honeycombs into a sticky pulp. Pour the resulting mixture of honey and wax into the paint strainer in the second bucket. With the help of gravity, over the course of several hours, honey will seep through the strainer out the holes you drilled in the second bucket and into the third bucket. After gravity has had a chance to do its thing, wax will remain in the strainer and all

the honey can now be poured into containers through the nifty, plastic spigot called the "honey gate." Honey doesn't have to be processed at all—you can eat it straight from the comb! Once it's poured in jars and sealed up, it will be ready to eat without fear of it ever spoiling.[1] The unique chemical composition of honey makes it inhospitable to microbial life and nothing can survive in it long enough to cause it to spoil. This is why honey is thought to have an eternal shelf life. Archeologist of the future will be able to dig up your honey and help themselves to some ancient sweetness![2]

1   Bees naturally cap off the comb when honey reaches a moisture level around 17 to 18 percent. If honey is processed while the moisture content is above 19.5 percent, it will likely ferment.

2   smithsonianmag.com/science-nature/the-science-behind-honeys-eternal-shelf-life-1218690/?no-ist

Depending on the plants bees visited, each batch of honey will vary in color, aroma and texture.

HONEY TASTE AND VARIATION

Honey is universally cherished for its sweetness, but the full flavor is much more complex and varies depending on the floral sources visited by the bees. Each plant bees visit produces nectar in differing quantities and qualities, and the resulting honey varies in color, aroma and texture. Honey ranges from transparent "water white" to the color of molasses, with amber as the median hue on the spectrum. The complex aromas of honey that contribute to its taste span from floral and fruity to medicinal or fermented. Raw or unpasteurized honey will naturally crystallize over time, which often misleads people into thinking that it has spoiled or gone bad. Crystallization affects the texture of honey, but preserves the flavor and aroma of the liquid honey. The rate that honey crystallizes depends on the nectar source, but pollen and wax in the honey helps catalyze the reaction. Crystallized honey can be reliquified for ease of use by heating the jar in a bath of warm water or setting it out in the sun.[1]

Beekeepers who move their bees for pollination or between honey flows can more easily pinpoint the "single source" of nectar their bees visited. These beekeepers can market their varietal honey to consumers who are eager for more information about the origins of their food. For example, a beekeeper harvesting from hives placed in an orange grove for pollination can market the resulting crop as orange-blossom honey. This marketing tactic du jour is used partially out of convenience for migratory beekeepers and in part to satisfy incredibly taste-specific parameters for chefs, foodies and picky eaters everywhere.

In recent years however, the question has become less about what the honey tastes like and more about where the honey comes from. The perceived benefits for allergy sufferers has driven the conversation toward valuing local honey above all else. Honey containing local pollen sources is thought to provide some relief from allergies. Beekeepers should steer clear of making claims that their honey provides any kind of

1   www.montcobeekeepers.org/Documents/Honey_Crystallization.pdf

Honey Harvest Mistakes

There are certain lessons in beekeeping that you only have to learn once, and bees have an effective way to help us learn from our mistakes. And as is often the case with beekeeping, sometimes we can learn more from our failures and mistakes than from our successes and good fortune. When it comes to harvesting honey, there are numerous ways you can screw things up, such as harvesting too much honey, provoking a defensive response and so on. Generally, most issues arise from the process of removing honey from the hive. The problems that pop up after the honey is out of the hive tend to create sticky messes.

After harvesting over 50 pounds of honey from our most prolific hive and leaving at least double that for the bees, I was jubilant as I returned home with the haul. Grinning ear to ear, I could hardly wait for a taste of the eucalyptus honey that was fueling the hive's impressive growth. I eagerly began assembling my crush-and-strain setup the minute I was inside. Having made some pretty impressive messes in past honey harvests, I was careful to cover the table I would use with butcher paper to catch the honey that was sure to drip everywhere. Once you cut the combs from the frames into the crushing bucket, the frame continues to drip honey until gravity takes its course. The butcher paper helps with cleanup, and helps me feed more of the honey back to the bees.

Everything was all set, and I cut the combs into the bucket and crushed them into a pulp of honey and wax. I had the two buckets for straining and collecting the honey set up on the ground, and I began pouring the honey pulp into the straining bucket. The honey from this hive had a high viscosity and is practically crystallized in the comb, which is my personal favorite, so pouring it into the straining bucket was quite a slow process. Once I filled the strainer to the brim, I took a break to let gravity work its magic.

I had planned on taking a good long break before bottling the honey. I happened to return to the kitchen a short while later to retrieve my phone so I could catch up on the text messages and calls I couldn't respond to while in a bee suit. Eager to see how much honey had already accumulated in the bottom bucket, I instantly recognized my blunder as honey flowed out of the open spigot onto our kitchen floor. After blurting out a series of colorful expletives, I dove to the ground to close the spigot and save the precious honey. Unfortunately, no matter how quickly I reacted, I couldn't help losing a good half-gallon of honey to the five-second rule. Even though honey is so anti-microbial I could have eaten every drop of it off of the floor without consuming a single harmful bacteria, try explaining that to your wife after she catches you slurping honey from the ground.

After trying to remedy the ordeal with more expletives and expressions of disbelief, I sheepishly called Chelsea to the kitchen for her appraisal of the situation. In the most compassionate way possible, she had a nice long laugh at my expense. "Bet you won't do that again!" she added with a smirk.

There was no use crying over spilled honey. We scooped whatever honey we could into a bowl and easily mopped up the rest. Rather than ditching the honey or feeding people "floor honey," we decided to take a page out of Cleopatra's book and use it for skin care and as shampoo. To this day, before I even think about harvesting honey, I make sure the spigot is closed and then I double check just to be sure. That is one lesson I only needed to learn once.

medicinal benefits, but can safely tout the benefits of buying locally produced food to the economy and the sustainability of our food supply. Plus, the local territory influences the unique taste of local honey and makes it preferable to the single source varietals produced in faraway fields, orchards, groves and patches. Thanks to the incredible diversity of floral sources found throughout our cities, the taste of honey from urban hives can be noticeably different from one neighborhood to the next.

By far the most popular HoneyLove workshop year after year is our honey tasting event. We select some of the world's finest and most sought after types of honey—from New Zealand's famous Manuka honey and Florida's Tupelo honey to French Lavender honey and Tuscan Acacia honey—and invite Los Angeles's urban beekeepers and HoneyLovers from all over the globe to contribute their honey for a blind taste test. Each variety of honey is set out next to a number, and tasters are given no further insights about the honey or clues about its origin. Each participant is given a numbered ballot to write down what strikes them about each variety and vote for their top three favorites.

We tally up the votes by awarding three points for each first place vote, two points for each second place vote and one point for each third place vote. Every year without fail, the honey from urban hives in Los Angeles is always among the top three, while the expensive, imported honey seldomly ranks high among voters. So far it has been a battle between Mar Vista, Culver City and Silver Lake for the title of best urban honey in Los Angeles. There also must be something going on in Colorado, as a HoneyLover and top-bar beekeeper from Aurora keeps taking top honors with her crystal-clear Linden and wildflower honey. We attribute the success of urban honey to the multitude of floral sources bees can visit within their foraging radius in a city. We think people prefer the complex tastes of the honey that results from this floral diversity. We like to think of urban honey as an orchestra of flavors playing a symphony together and compare varietal honey to a single musician playing one note, as beautiful as it may be, again and again on his own.

Forager bee on lavender flower (Left)

Urban Beekeeping Basics for Tiny and Giant Backyards

The fundamentals of beekeeping are the same regardless of location; however, there are some unique considerations when keeping bees in an urban or suburban environment.

A NEW GENERATION OF BEEKEEPERS

The unprecedented explosion in the popularity of urban and backyard beekeeping has reinvigorated an industry once demoralized by varroa mites, economic pressures and failure to replenish its ranks with new generations of beekeepers.

The surge of new beekeepers is partially in response to the global alarm bells resonating throughout the media warning of an imminent collapse of bee populations. Fears of colony collapse disorder have propelled the issues beekeepers have been grappling with for decades into news headlines, documentaries and dinner table discussions like never before. Seen as indicators of environmental health, the collapse of honeybee colonies serves as a dire warning of an invisible and unknown threat to our lives.

The gloom and doom predictions of a future devoid of bees served as inspiration and a call to action for people all over the world to take up beekeeping. It is too early to fully understand the effect this influx of new beekeepers has had on the populations of honeybees, but it is fairly safe to say that the infusion of optimism, youth and new energy into the hobby, in tandem with the impressive number of women entering the fray, has saved one of the most endangered species: the beekeeper.

Prior to the modern beekeeping resurgence, the average demographic for beekeepers was males in their 50s and 60s, and the industry as a whole struggled to find new blood willing to take on the challenges, risks and lifestyle necessary to keep bees. While the difficulties that go along with being a beekeeper—especially as a primary means of income—remain basically the same, an entire new generation has been seduced by the hive and stricken with "bee fever." This new crop of beekeepers will yield the new ideas, perspectives and solutions needed to carry beekeeping forward to feed future generations.

Technology is another big reason people are answering the call to become beekeepers in record numbers. Finally, after centuries of trying to share our love of bees with the masses, beekeepers are able to invite interested parties to join us in visiting with our bees—all from the comfort of a smartphone or laptop. At last people finally get what we've been talking about, and all it took was a handheld device that can record high-definition video and instantly broadcast it to a global audience. Social media has inspired legions of new beekeepers with mesmerizing images from within the hive and tantalizing shots of delicious honey. Fortunately, learning about bees has never been easier through online forums and abundant educational resources available for free. Urban beekeepers can now start learning how to keep their bees healthy from the comfort of their own living rooms.

THE CASE FOR URBAN BEEKEEPING

Before getting into beekeeping you have to realize that not everyone shares your profound admiration of bees. In fact, for many people, bees are terrifying and loathsome creatures. The idea of keeping bees in close proximity is seen as lunacy and perceived as dangerous.

Considering the majority of people throughout history were at least partially responsible for providing their own fruit and produce, *not* keeping bees would have been seen as risky and ill-advised until relatively recently. As our populations soar and our resources grow scarce, the need to better integrate food production into our population centers grows more important by the day. Local food production is a pillar of sustainability;

Bees arriving home from foraging (Right)

populations of the future cannot be fed by further expansion of agricultural lands. Genetic engineering, pesticides and chemical fertilizers are unlikely to account for the additional food the world must produce to feed its growing population.

Our food production model has had a profoundly negative impact on ecosystems and the biodiversity of our planet. There exists a partially substantiated mythology that it would be impossible to feed the earth's population any other way, in large part thanks to short-term yield gains derived from use of chemicals. An increasing body of research dismisses this as myth, with evidence suggesting little or no yield benefit over traditional organic practices that rely on tremendous diversity of plant species, microbes in the soil and pollinators in the air.[1]

In addition to finding ways to minimize agriculture's impact on ecosystems, special effort must be put toward making food systems more durable and resilient. This means growing more of our food where we live and promoting biodiversity in our food systems. Urban beekeeping presents a special opportunity to work toward making our cities more sustainable and improving our food security.

"I think urban beekeeping is very exciting. In our work with pesticides, we have limited data but the data is exciting...we found that the pesticide load in urban colonies typically is far less than commercial hives that are being used for pollination. We have been excited about the lack of pesticides that we have seen in urban areas, so we are very, very thankful for that... I think urban beekeeping is very exciting and hugely important."

—Maryann Frazier, honeybee researcher and senior extension associate of Penn State University

Between gardens, landscaping, parks, green spaces, wild areas and even the weeds growing through cracks in the cement, cities offer bees an abundance of forage from a large variety of floral sources. Honeybee colonies prosper in urban environments due to this nutritional advantage, and in exchange, they pollinate the local plants that beautify our homes, produce food and produce oxygen.

1   huffingtonpost.com/eric-holt-gimenez/agroecology-and-the-disappearing-yield-gap_b_6290982.html

BEEKEEPING DIPLOMACY

The only problem for honeybees in urban environments is humans, which makes it incumbent upon urban beekeepers to exercise the diplomacy necessary to help wed city-loving bees and sting-weary humans. Urban beekeepers are diplomats first and beekeepers second. All the beekeeping knowledge and skill in the world do little to calm neighbors' nerves upon discovering a newly installed beehive. Beekeeping diplomacy is no small challenge, but by following best practices, exercising extreme precaution and winning a little goodwill, urban beekeepers can be seen as real assets to their communities.

Gaining the respect and trust of the community will vary from person to person, town to town and so on. Unfortunately, there isn't any fail-safe procedure or game plan for winning support for urban beekeeping in your community. However, you do have honey to help sweeten any deal, and you can provide a tremendous service to people in need of assistance when swarms show up. These two things can go a long way toward winning the support of your neighbors and community members.

If you have poor relationships with your neighbors, you may find that adding bees to the equation does little to help patch things up. Unfortunately, urban beekeepers have had to relinquish their hives—after spending hundreds of dollars setting them up—in the face of threats of legal escalation from neighbors. Consulting with city zoning codes and following them closely is the best strategy for avoiding any potential legal proceedings. In the absence of laws permitting or prohibiting beekeeping, you should consider pushing your local city council to legalize it.[1]

---

1   For more resources about legalizing beekeeping in your community, please visit HoneyLove.org/Resources.

Dr. Noah Wilson-Rich, founder and chief scientific officer of The Best Bees Company, in an article written for the HoneyLove blog writes, "City planners must remain forward-thinking. California is a huge agricultural state. To make any pollinators illegal is to limit agriculture. That decreases job availability, limits food production and prevents access to education. These are social justice issues, and policy makers must take action to allow access to these resources for all residents. In 100 years, is it possible that we could have modern, urban farms on rooftops or underutilized properties? It is, if policy allows it so. Our population is growing, but our available land is not. We must be smart about how we plan for the future of urban living."[1]

1   HoneyLove.org/should-la-legalize-beekeeping/

In service of preventing unwanted attention, many beekeepers attempt to conceal their bees in any number of clever ways. Many beekeepers subscribe to the "I'd rather beg for forgiveness than ask for permission" model, but sometimes even the best efforts at camouflaging hives can go sideways. Neighbors might not see the hive or the bees, but they are likely to notice the beekeeper's astronaut-like suit or the plumes of smoke rising from the backyard or rooftop. In the long run, it pays to be diplomatic and warm up neighbors to the idea of bees next door.

You should make special efforts to address any concerns, demonstrate the precautionary measures taken to prevent problems and outline the course of action to be taken in the unlikely event the bees must be removed from the location. Neighbors and especially their kids are often eager to learn about bees, and you are encouraged to have an extra suit or two on hand so you can invite others to participate in installations, inspections and of course, honey harvests. Sharing the adventure of beekeeping and being generous with honey is a great way for you to earn the support of your neighbors.

Catching swarms (see p. 68) is another great way beekeepers can give back to their community. *You* know that swarms are harmless, but to the majority of people the sight of tens of thousands of bees in the air is terrifying. The appearance of swarms generally results in panicked calls to vector control or animal services. You can contact these services and volunteer to be on-call for swarms, and often city staffers are eager to leave the job to someone with proper training who will not kill the bees. Showing up at the scene of a disrupted Little League game or backyard birthday or wherever a swarm may appear is the beekeeper's time to shine! You get to look like a bee-whispering hero, *and* you get a new colony of bees! That's a win-win! Once the diplomatic offensive has been set in motion, you can get back to the good stuff and focus on your bees.

WHERE TO LOCATE YOUR HIVE

One of the first questions to be answered if you're considering urban beekeeping is where you will situate the hive. Check with local city ordinances for guidelines concerning proximity to property lines and other regulations governing where you can place bees on your property. Most city or county ordinances about beekeeping are land use regulations: whether or not beekeeping is permitted, and if so, under which conditions. These regulations usually govern how many hives are permitted, how far they must be from neighboring properties or public rights-of-way, the direction the hive entrance must face and whether the beekeeper must install water sources and maintain flyway barriers.[1] Issues like genetics, requeening, required treatments and other management issues cannot logistically be enforced at the city level and should only be issued as

---

1 Flyway barriers can include a wall, solid fence or dense vegetation, depending on your city's definition.

There are fewer safety considerations for keeping bees in agricultural settings. (Left)

guidelines if at all. These topics are best discussed among beekeepers in forums and meetings, at conventions and in journals; lawmakers with little to no beekeeping experience should not be deciding what's best for honeybees.

As with every aspect of urban beekeeping, the human element is the primary variable. It's important to think through hive and human interaction possibilities, such as whether the meter reader or delivery person will have to walk by the hive, or whether the hive may be in jeopardy of being toppled by incoming soccer balls. When evaluating a location's worthiness, you must ensure that the bees' flight path will not intersect with busy human walkways.

Bees take off from and land on the hive following the same basic trajectory, called the beeline. The arrivals and departures appear as if their flight patterns are being radioed in from air traffic control. You can use physical barriers like hedges or shade cloth fences as "flyways" to divert the beeline away from human pathways. If possible, the best locations are tucked far away from any foot traffic in a seldom-visited portion of the yard where bees can come and go as they please.

Bees have a tendency to take offense to lawn mowers and weed whackers, so the farther away the hive is placed from these activities the better. In addition to being irritated by the vibrations and noise, bees are also influenced by communication pheromones released when plants are disturbed. Some plants have been shown to use pheromones to communicate with members of the same species to signal distress as a result of insect infestation or being grazed upon by any number of vegetarian species looking to fill their bellies. Presumably these chemical pheromones are used to ward off pests and discourage the plant's destruction. Bees are likely sensitive to these pheromones and take issue with the noisy contraption causing all the ruckus. If the hive feels sufficiently

In the event the bees begin chasing people, beekeepers should quickly get their suits on, fire up their smokers and make the air around the hive thick with smoke. The smoke will help dissipate and disrupt the alarm pheromone responsible for the bees' defensive behavior. Continue to pump the smoke until things have settled down, but be careful not to further agitate the bees by making the inside of the hive too smoky. Even the angriest hive should settle down after ten or twenty minutes of proper smoking—beekeepers may know humans for which this is also true.

threatened by the mower, guard bees are likely to go looking for someone to blame.

ROOFTOP HIVES

Urban beekeepers commonly place hives on flat roofs, high above foot traffic and far away from vandals, soccer balls, pets and pesticides. Rooftop hives and gardens are a great way to turn underutilized urban areas into pockets of food production, which in turn helps improve the food security of our cities. Rooftop beekeepers must be aware of the possibility of having to move their bees to a new location, a task that becomes exponentially more challenging if ladders are involved. Empty hive boxes that went up the ladder with ease get quickly packed with bees and honey, soon weighing between 50 and 75 pounds each, making the trip down the ladder significantly more precarious.

Having an exit strategy that accounts for the tremendous heft of a successful beehive, preferably one that avoids ladders, is a must for rooftop hives. Ladders are probably the most dangerous part of beekeeping, and should be used cautiously and judiciously. Whether it's stretching from the top rung to catch a swarm high in a tree or hoisting honey supers down from rooftop hives, there is no mission worth risking broken bones. From locations to ladders, safety and caution should be layered into every aspect of urban beekeeping.

WATER SOURCES

Providing an adequate water source is a must for all beekeepers, especially so for those keeping bees in urban and highly populated areas. While bees will have no trouble finding water in these environments, you are encouraged to put out a water source before installing a new hive in the hope that they will prefer it over your neighbor's pool, hose bib or anywhere people may object to their presence.

Saltwater pools are especially attractive to honeybees, a common complaint among owners of the chlorine-alternative pools. Honeybees have hair-like receptors on the bottoms of their feet that allow them to "taste" their environment. They are presumably attracted to these pools for a salty treat for their feet, so to speak. Those who have unwittingly tramped on a bee barefoot at the beach likely did so because the offending bee was there for a sip and a snack.

Once bees decide upon a preferred source, they will continue to visit it as long as there is water available. Having the water source in place before the bees arrive is the best strategy for getting them to orient to the desired source. Bees are terrible swimmers and can be clumsy in their attempts to gather water. Aquatic plants make excellent landing pads, corks and floating sticks also work to help prevent bees from falling in the water and drowning.

It is critically important that water sources not be allowed to become stagnant as they can become a source for bloodsucking, disease-transmitting mosquitoes. Whether or not mosquitoes in your area harbor infectious diseases, there is no reason to maintain a breeding ground for humanity's most despised creature—next to the varroa mite of course. The best way to prevent this from happening is to use a water pump to keep water circulating throughout the vessel. Pumps need electricity, but inexpensive solar panels can provide sufficient power to keep water flowing even at off-grid bee yards. If you can be assured your water source cannot escape or spill into larger waterways, introducing certain species of fish that prey on mosquito larvae is a way to reduce mosquito populations. These fish can be invasive and wreak havoc in native ecosystems, so you should not employ this method if there is any chance they could spread from the water source to local waterways. The same is true for a number of aquatic plants used in aquariums and ponds that would otherwise make perfect landing strips for thirsty bees.

SWARMING AND THE CITY

The sudden arrival of tens of thousands of bees is not always instinctively a welcome experience for urban dwellers and typically results in frantic calls to city services, pest control operators or beekeepers. Even though they are generally harmless, swarms can be disruptive and inspire a great deal of fear. Swarms looking for a cavity space to colonize often take refuge in buildings and man-made structures, and removing colonies from these locations is labor intensive and can require expensive repairs. Urban beekeepers must make a special effort to prevent their bees from swarming to maintain goodwill in the community.

To prevent overcrowding, it is important for beekeepers to routinely inspect their hives every two to three weeks in the spring and catch colonies preparing to swarm. Capped queen cells are a telltale sign the colony is days from swarming. Hives make queen cups as placeholders for future queen cells. These can be easily missed without close inspection. Look carefully to confirm that queen cells are occupied by developing larvae before concluding the hive is about to swarm. Upon discovering occupied queen cells, the best option for urban beekeepers is to simulate a swarm by making splits. Swarm boxes make an excellent second line of defense for urban beekeepers to prevent their bees from swarming and taking up residence in a neighbor's wall or water meter. (See Chapter 6 – How to Save a Failing Hive, p. 111.)

A swarm of honeybees is not always welcome in an urban community, so beekeepers should try to prevent their bees from swarming. (Right)

CHAPTER 11

The Art of Beekeeping

There is no one right way to keep bees; there is only the way that works best for you. Finding and fine-tuning your unique beekeeping approach is an art. Rather than looking for hard and fast rules, I encourage you to look at beekeeping as an artistic *process*, in which you find the best answers for you and your bees. Like any art, beekeeping is learned through repetition over a lifetime; no set of facts, activities, tactics or procedures can be listed and memorized. As an art form, there isn't a right or correct way to keep bees, in the same way that there is not a right or wrong way for artists to express themselves with paint. Some artists mix their own paints and hand paint their visions on canvas they stretched themselves, others make a statement by spraying their paint on "found" canvases made of bricks and cement, while others use digital paint brushes on pixelated canvas to create their visions in three dimensions. Art critics can factor in the methods artists use to express themselves, but a piece of art's beauty and emotional resonance are far more influential as critics decide whether it is a quality work of art or total crap.

In the art of beekeeping, the hive is the canvas, our management style is the paint and the health of our bees is our artwork. The only critics that beekeepers should pay any attention to are their bees. If your hives are giving you two thumbs up and are as healthy as can be, then keep doing whatever you're doing. If your bees are struggling and failing to thrive, you need to take a closer look at what role you are playing in their poor health. Beekeeping is a balancing act between knowing when to intervene and when it's time to remember the ninth principle of beekeeping backwards—leave your bees alone.

The first thing that I should have mentioned before spouting off my opinions and beliefs is that I deeply respect all beekeepers regardless of how they practice apiculture. Getting bent out of shape because someone does or doesn't chemically treat their bees is a waste of time. All you can do is find common ground in the fact that we all love our bees and want them to be healthy and productive.

Now that you have finished reading this book, let me dispel any illusion that I am or claim to be an expert on bees or beekeeping. I don't have any kind of special recipe for beekeeping that is universally applicable. There is so much about honeybees that remains a mystery; just when you think you've wrapped your head around your bees, something else

will pop up that makes you question everything you think you know. The joke among beekeepers is that the bees didn't read our books on beekeeping.

I encourage beekeepers to have an open mind, and I really caution you to avoid ideological purity when it comes to your approach to beekeeping. Do not limit the ideas and perspectives you are willing to entertain. Be weary of beekeepers peddling their "expertise" because nobody has *all* the answers, *but* they might be able to teach you a thing or two. You should always keep an open mind and leap at any opportunity you get to connect with other beekeepers. Even beekeepers who have dramatically opposing views can learn something from each other. In fact, I think that the greater the difference two beekeepers' management practices are, the more time they should spend teaching each other about their style and why it works.

I chose treatment-free beekeeping because it resonated with my personal ethos and worldview. I believe it has the greatest potential to positively impact honeybees and the health of our environment. However, that hasn't stopped me from learning important lessons from beekeepers who consider chemically treating their bees much like taking children to the doctor when they are sick. By their logic, not treating our bees doesn't make sense and borders on cruelty. *We don't think twice about treating our dogs for fleas when they can't stop scratching themselves, so why shouldn't we do the same with our bees even though they are insects and it's harder to notice their suffering?* For my friends who treat their hives, loving their bees means helping them survive by any means necessary.

The bottom line is we *all* love our bees and are fiercely protective of our hives. That's enough common ground for me to make friends with and learn from beekeepers from all walks of life. The greatest lesson I've learned from these friendships is that, to be a successful beekeeper, you have to keep your bees in a way that rhymes with the way you look at the world and use methods that align with your life's philosophy. Otherwise, it's not possible to uphold Kirkobeeo's eleventh principle of beekeeping backwards—beekeeping should be fun!

It would be utterly impossible to catalog every possible beekeeping scenario and shell out advice that applies to every situation while factoring in the appropriate context. There is no way this or any book can spell out every solution for every issue that pops up in beekeeping. Instead, my hope is that this book will help you begin to think like a beekeeper, and equip you with a knowledge "toolbox" to pull from and help you make decisions, solve problems and learn from your bees. As you gain experience with your bees, you will develop the ability to do basic beekeeping algebra. By factoring all of the

variables into the equation and applying the basic beekeeping formula outlined in this book, you can solve whatever issues may pop up in a hive. You will also use the same basic toolbox to assess and analyze what you did right with your hive when it flourishes and what you may have done wrong when a colony fails to thrive. Beekeeping is all about trial and error, you should not be afraid to fail, because making mistakes is one of the most important parts of the learning process. If you pay close attention and learn from the times you mess up, your bees will teach you everything you need to know about beekeeping—and life!

When you look at a hive as a beekeeper you can't help but try to make sense of what you are seeing. Your mind almost subconsciously starts looking for patterns to explain how the systems work, and the intrigue only grows stronger with time as you discover more and more about bees. The type of thinking you engage in while studying your bees' behavior—system thinking—spills over into all aspects of your life and greatly influences how you view the world. You can't witness and understand the complexity of the hive ecology and the importance of bees and pollinators to the greater ecosystem and not start thinking about your world a little differently than before you started beekeeping. Immediately after introducing bees into your backyard and life, your garden suddenly extends at least four miles in any direction. Even though you may not use pesticides or fungicides in your garden and landscaping, your bees can encounter them anywhere in their massive foraging flight, which can reach over 32,000 acres.[1] If you didn't realize how closely tied we are to our environment before, beekeeping has a way of connecting the dots and making that point hit a little closer to home. This is why we need more beekeepers, especially urban and backyard beekeepers, to help create cleaner, more sustainable cities that are healthier for humans and honeybees.

I'm so glad that I noticed the swarm that spring day. Now I can't imagine my life without bees. Chelsea and I feel so lucky to have fallen into a community of beekeepers in Los Angeles who share our desire to keep bees in the most natural way possible without the use of harmful chemicals. Every time I see Kirk Anderson, I try to say thank you for helping me get into bees and for inspiring us to create HoneyLove. One of the biggest lessons I've learned from Kirk is the importance of passing the torch and helping others discover the magic and mystery of honeybees. Now that I have shared all I know about beekeeping, your job as a beekeeper is to tell anyone who will listen all about bees. You never know what kind of spark you might create in someone's life. My hope is that you will continue to read and learn about bees, take in all kinds of perspectives, resist confirmation bias and be open to ideas and solutions even if they challenge what you think you know.

1   www.beesource.com/point-of-view/joe-traynor/how-far-do-bees-fly-one-mile-two-seven-and-why/

You learn something new every time you open a hive—never stop learning! (Right)

ACKNOWLEDGMENTS

To the countless beekeepers who continue to inspire us: Kirk Anderson, Michael Bush, Michael Thiele, Les Crowder, Dee Lusby, Bill Lewis, Noah Wilson-Rich, Sam Comfort, Sarah Red-Laird, Eliese Watson, Matt Reed, Bob Redmond and Maryann Frazier.

And to our many dear friends, family members and HoneyLovers who have supported us throughout the years, we are truly in your debt! Special thanks to Ceebs Bailey, Paul Hekimian, George Langworthy, Susan Rudnicki, Kevin O'Scanlon, Dennis Broderick, Barry & Ashley Fontenot, Sean & Anne Marie Austin, Amy Long, Nicholas Austin, Debra Erickson, Meredith Hackleman, Pearl Gottschalk, Bill Rosendahl, Mike Bonin, Walker Rollins, Roberta Kato, Erik Knutzen, Ruth Askren, Maritza Przekop, Sherri Akers, David King, Andy Shrader, Martin Schlageter, Bryce Kunzel, Kendra Tarte, Patricia Anderson and Page Street Publishing!

Rob McFarland, since early childhood, has always had a passion and interest in wildlife. Known for spending his days exploring the neighborhood ponds in Spokane, WA, he loved wading in the water to check out the local turtles and frogs. After graduating college from Eastern Washington University, Rob volunteered with the Orangutan Foundation International and set off for Borneo, Indonesia, to help create GIS maps of Tanjung Puting National Park. The goal of the trip was to gather land-cover data that could be used to assess how much of the park had been degraded by fires, deforestation, palm oil plantations and human settlements. This meant hiking throughout the park's peat swamp forests to characterize the land cover and log observations with handheld GPS devices and a video camera.

Chelsea McFarland grew up in a California beach community and was raised to value and protect the environment. In sixth grade she read John Robbin's *Diet for a New America*, and was inspired to become a vegetarian. In keeping with her Californian roots, technology played a major role in her childhood. Finding herself on the first wave of Internet adopters, Chelsea quickly developed a skill set that gave her creative freedom and the ability to connect with people all over the world. By college she decided to channel her technical skills and passion for storytelling toward a career in filmmaking. After graduating from the University of California, Santa Cruz, Chelsea set off on her own to explore India and document cultural dances in the most remote regions of the subcontinent.

Rob and Chelsea were set up while traveling in Asia as travel companions and to create a PSA with Rob's footage from Borneo for the Orangutan Foundation International. After working together, Rob and Chelsea returned home to the United States as a couple and started building their careers in media and technology. In 2011, the McFarlands founded HoneyLove as a Los Angeles based 501(c)3 nonprofit conservation organization with a mission to protect the honeybees by educating our communities and inspiring new urban beekeepers. For more information, visit HoneyLove.org.

INDEX

round veil, *46*

Rudnicki, Susan, 53

S

safety considerations, beekeeping in agricultural settings, *162*

ScientificBeekeeping.com, 104

scout bees, 66

Seeley, Dr. Thomas, 66

shallows frames, 33

shim, 130

Silver Lake, 155

Simon, Charles Martin, 19

    ten principles of beekeeping backwards, 20

small hive beetles (SHB), 107–108

Smith, Dr. Maurice V., 30

smoker, 28, *48*, 50–53, 90–91

    firestarter for, *51*

    use of for thousands of years, *52*

solid laying pattern, *99*

splits, making, 117–119

starter strips, 28

Stiglitz, Dean, 20

straining bucket

    holes drilled in, *148*

    paint strainer in, *147*

    placed on bottom bucket, *148*

    wrapping duct tape around paint strainer in, *147*

sugar shakes, 103

superorganism, 76–78

swarm, 60, 65–73, 65–73

    of honeybees, *65, 167*

    how to catch, 68–69

    swarm boxes, 69–71

swarm boxes, *71*

swarming

    preventing, 120–121

    urban beekeeping and, 166

swarms

    decisions made by, 66

T

Tanglefoot, 60

Thiele, Michael, 20

Top-Bar beekeeping, 30

Top-Bar Beekeeping: Organic Practices for Honeybee Health (Les Crowder), 30

Top-Bar Hive, 30, 31

    with naturally drawn comb, *31*

    with observation window, *30*

Townsend, Dr. Gordon, 30

treatment-free beekeepers, 16, 105

    Beekeeping Backwards, 19–21

    Charles Martin Simon's Ten Principles of Beekeeping Backwards, 20–21

    inspecting the hive, *17*

    principles of, 15–22

    saving the bees and, 15–22

understanding bees, 21–22

treatment-free beekeeping, 13, 15

Tupelo honey (Florida), 155

U

University of Guelph (Canada), 30

urban beekeepers

    in Los Angeles, 20

    winning support for, 161

urban beekeeping

    basics for small and large backyards, 157–166

    basics of, 165

    beekeeping diplomacy, 161, 163

    the case for, 158, 160

    a new generation of beekeepers, 157–158

    rooftop hives, 165

    swarming and, 166

    water sources, 165–166

    where to locate your hive, 163–165

USDA, 21

V

Vanishing of the Bees (documentary directed by George Langworthy), 13

varroa mites, 13, 15, 103–104, 128, 157

American hives and, 103

drones and, 106

inspecting for, 103–104

negative effect of treatment and, 107

treatment with chemicals, 104

veil

domed hood, *46*

fencing, *46*

round, *46*

veiled pith helmets, *44*, 45

von Frisch, Karl, 66, 78

W

water sources, in urban beekeeping, 165–166

wax moths, 109

Achroia grisell, 109

Galleria mellonella, 109

inspecting for, 109

wax secretion, 82, 84

weatherproofing, 28

supplies for, *38*

Wilson-Rich, Dr. Noah, 161

worker bees, 82, *82, 87*